Also By Judge Swann

The Techniques of Softening: E.T.A. Hoffmann's Presentation of the Fantastic, 1971, Yale University Press

Five Proofs of Christianity, 2016, Westbow Press

Politics, Faith, and Love, 2017, Balboa Press

Kirksey, 2021, Balboa Press

More Kirksey, 2021, Balboa Press

The Judith Files, 2021, Balboa Press

These are available from the publishers, and from Amazon.

WHAT IF?

JUDGE BILL SWANN

BALBOA.PRESS
A DIVISION OF HAY HOUSE

Balboa Press books may be ordered through booksellers or by contacting:

Balboa Press
A Division of Hay House
1663 Liberty Drive
Bloomington, IN 47403
www.balboapress.com
844-682-1282

Print information available on the last page.

ISBN: 979-8-7652-3542-3 (sc)
ISBN: 979-8-7652-3544-7 (hc)
ISBN: 979-8-7652-3543-0 (e)

Library of Congress Control Number: 2022918779

Balboa Press rev. date: 12/07/2022

Contents

Dedication

This book is dedicated to Christopher, my oldest son. He started me down this track of thought. He has always thought "outside the box," as the saying goes, and now he has me doing it.

The phrase comes from this problem: Connect nine dots which are arranged in a square, using only four continuous straight lines.

You can do it, but it cannot be done without drawing outside the box.

Personas

Everything written, fiction and nonfiction, has a personality behind it. The creating personality. A reader will come to a conclusion about this creating personality. He or she is brittle. Or perhaps biased. Or again, arrogant, or likable, and so on.

In the writing trade, this is called a "persona."

This is not to be confused with the "person" talking. That may be in the first person, that is, written in the "I" voice. I did this, I did that, and the like.

Or again in the second person, the "you" voice. The writer addresses the reader directly.

Or in the third person: "Kirksey was walking at Lakeshore Park when he saw . . ."

In this book, you will find all three persons used. But as to me, the "persona" behind the text, I hope you will find me likable.

Acknowledgements

I give thanks to Christopher Hogin (JD, MDiv), for his help on "Giving Tree" and "Cat's in the Cradle." Christopher is the son of my former law partner John Hogin.

I also thank John Harber for his help with "The Buffalo Nickel." I had never heard of the 1828 Tennessee, Georgia, and North Carolina gold rush. Thus I also knew nothing of Bechtler gold.

I thank Matt Suddath for his help on "What if the NFL introduces flexible field length?"

And I thank Bob Swan for his help on "What if all the TVA dams vanished?"

What if you couldn't hear?

KIRKSEY WAS IN GATLINBURG. WHEN HE WOKE UP HE NOTICED THE birds were not singing. He went into the kitchen. "Alexa," he said, "what's the weather?" Alexa's light came on, but she didn't say anything. That's funny, he thought. He turned on the TV, channel 787. They were there, the Fox News people, talking, but not making any noise. He picked up a pan and dropped it on the floor. Not a sound. This is serious, he thought. I'm deaf.

He tried one more time. "Alexa, play KSL Salt Lake." Alexa's light came on, but he heard nothing. This is not good, he said to himself.

He made tea, added milk, rewarmed it in the microwave and sat down to breakfast. It was still dark outside. Kirksey couldn't tell whether the bear had come or not. Probably not. Well, Kirksey thought, even if he had been here last night, I guess I wouldn't have heard him.

He got out his iPhone, found text messages, and sent a short,. "Good morning, love, how are you?" to Diana. She wouldn't be awake yet. When she called back, he wouldn't hear her. But his phone would vibrate, so he would know she was sending something.

Kirksey had been trying out a pair of hearing aids. It was funny how that industry worked, or at least the audiology practice he was going to. They gave you a hearing assessment and if you showed a hearing loss, which Kirksey did, they offered you a trial pair. "Take them home, see what you think."

Kirksey had taken the little things, gotten instructions on how to use them, and downloaded a phone app to control them.

He had had the hearing aids for two weeks now, and they were great. He heard crickets and birds in the morning as he walked at Lakeshore Park. He heard the flights of geese in the distance. Previously he had only heard them when they were close. It was terrific. The hearing aids enriched his life. He even thought they improved his vision, which was silly.

He thought, "Let's put on the hearing aids this morning and see if they make any difference." They didn't. This was bad. He really was deaf.

Diana sent him a text message. She said she couldn't hear anything, and that's why she was writing to him and had not called. Kirksey wrote back, "I know," he wrote. "Is there anything on the news?"

In a few minutes she wrote back. She said there was. "You can see the news people talking," she said, "but they must know we can't hear them, because everything they are saying is typed on the screen. Some of the news people are saying it's probably another Chinese virus."

As Kirksey's day went on, there were chyrons and lots of graphics. The news got out, it was just a different way to do it. He wrote back to Diana, "This is bad. What are we going to do?" "I don't think there's anything we can do," she wrote, "but I'd feel better if you came home." Kirksey said he would pack up and be there that afternoon.

THIRTY DAYS LATER

Kirksey had figured out a way to do his Zoom mediations. It was strange, but it worked. You still used breakout rooms, putting husband and his counsel in one room, wife and her counsel in another room, and himself and the two attorneys in a third room. Everybody typed everything. Or, if someone could not type, they wrote stuff on yellow legal pads and held it up to the camera. It was slower than Kirksey's mediations had been, but they got done. Kirksey's hourly time for each mediation was longer, so his cash flow had improved. That was definitely OK.

Diana could not read to Marren any more. But she turned the pages of books and used flashcards to teach Marren words. Reading was still going to be important for her, as it was for everyone. So Diana was working hard at that. All the schools we're teaching "word families" now. The "at family," for example, had "bat, cat, hat," and so forth. No one called it phonics now, because nothing was phonetic when you couldn't hear.

All the news was done in graphics. Most of the stations didn't even bother to have a talking head pretending to deliver the news.

Some people blamed the deafness on President Trump. The Democratic party said the Trump administration had done little for deafness disability. The Democrats would do anything, Kirksey thought, to keep Trump from getting re-elected in 2020.

The election itself was going to be interesting. Some people had wondered whether Joe Biden could hear even before the worldwide deafness occurred. Now that was moot.

As far as the airways were concerned, it was simply TV. No radio. The Wall Street Journal wrote that radio stations were being mothballed in hopes of better days. The mutual funds with communications corporations took a dip, probably never to recover, Kirksey thought.

There was no live music. But then, there was no music at all, anywhere. Not on the radio, not on TV, not in Knoxville's old city. Not even in Music City Nashville. Still, God bless capitalism, there was now a budding mime industry in Nashville, and beer was being sold hand-over-fist. Tootsie's Orchid Lounge on Broadway was doing well selling beer, even without music.

Kirksey had always liked beer joints, where they played country music on the jukebox, or played it live. There was no music now, of course.

"The singer plays for tips," said a cardboard handmade sign at Tootsie's. It was taped to a jar stuffed with dollar bills. Probably a pickled-egg jar once.

Kirksey had been gone a long time. Thirteen years. Boston, Munich, Austria, Berlin. Then Yale University for the degree, Brown University to teach. Then he had come back home, to Tennessee, to law school, to friends he had not known he had.

Kirksey wondered how people deaf from birth felt, now that everyone was deaf. He guessed some of them thought, "Now you see how we have been making it all along."

Probably there would soon be deaf-from-birth capitalists giving tutorials on how to cope.

What if you cannot read?

WHEN KIRKSEY WOKE UP HE WENT INTO THE KITCHEN TO SEE WHAT he had written down in the middle of the night. He couldn't read it. I'll get my glasses later, he thought. "Alexa," he said, "what's the weather?" "Today in Gatlinburg you can expect sun and thunderstorms with a low of 66 degrees and a high of 82 degrees." "Thank you, Alexa," he said. "You bet," she said.

Kirksey's little finger was sore on the right hand. He had dinged it yesterday and it looked like things were going downhill. It was surrounded by a small red ring. He went in the bathroom, found Diana's medical kit, and put Neosporin on the spot. He wrapped it in a Band-Aid. Wonder if it'll stay all day, he thought. Well, I can change it out if not. He went back to the kitchen. "Alexa, play KSL Salt Lake." "Today on the Wasatch Range there will be rain with a high of 70 degrees and a low of 45. The traffic at Midvale . . ."

He pulled up his emails on the iPad but he couldn't read them. Where are my glasses? Oh they must be over at the office. Nowadays with Covid-19 Kirksey was doing all his mediations by Zoom from the little house next door. That's what he called his office. Well, he would deal with email later. He finished making tea, added milk, rewarmed it in the microwave and sat down to cinnamon toast and ham. He listened to Steven Furtick on the iPad. It was a short sermon but long enough for breakfast. Furtick always put his biblical quotations on the screen, but Kirksey couldn't read them. That was okay because Furtick made clear what he was talking about.

Yesterday a bear had been across the street at one of the rental houses and pulled a bag of garbage out of the truck belonging to the cleaning crew. That was definitely getting old. This was about the eighth time it had happened. It meant that Kirksey had had to go out with his own garbage bag and pick up all the garbage the bear had distributed up the slope to the A-frame, the big house. Definitely getting old. It also meant Kirksey would have to post the notices again, not that the notices did much good. But then, he thought, he really couldn't tell how many disasters the notices had prevented. He always put the notices beside the door at each of the four houses. The sheet of paper asked the cleaning crews of the houses to keep their garbage secure so that Kirksey and Diana would not have to clean up the messes that resulted.

So, maybe the bear would come back today and Kirksey would find out whether he had grown tall enough to reach the new bird feeder system.

There were two kinds of bird seed: black sunflower which the bear really liked, and hot pepper seed cakes. The squirrels hated the hot seed cakes.

He made a second cup of tea, warmed it in the microwave, and carried it over to the little house, and found his glasses. He opened up the emails. He couldn't read them. What was going on?

He got out his iPhone, found the green bubble for text messages, and dictated a short good morning, love, how are you? to Diana. She wouldn't be awake yet. He wondered what was going on. His eyes were fine. He could see everything clearly. But he couldn't read his emails. Maybe it was just a computer thing. He picked up a volume of Tennessee Code Annotated. It didn't matter which code section. He just wanted to read the law, read anything. The page was a blur. Ah, shit, he said. This is weird. He hoped Diana would call back soon.

THIRTY DAYS LATER

Kirksey woke up. The national news had speculated that this reading thing was yet another Chinese viral agent, from Wuhan or wherever else the Chinese did their dirty biology. The Chinese of course denied it, but they could still read, so they probably had an antidote. Kirksey figured it was pretty open and shut that the Chinese had done this thing. He remembered how the Chinese had responded to their Wuhan-produced

Covid virus, shutting down flights from Wuhan to cities in China, but leaving Wuhan's international flights free to spread the virus.

Kirksey was at the big house in Gatlinburg. He was scheduled to do a Zoom mediation later in the day. He hadn't written himself a reminder note in the middle of the night because he knew he wouldn't be able to read it. He had told Alexa to remind him.

Kirksey walked into the kitchen. "Alexa, what's the weather?" "Today in Gatlinburg you can expect rain and thunderstorms with a high of 65 degrees and a low of 52 degrees. Have a good day, Bill." "Alexa, thank you." "Any time," she said. It was stupid that Kirksey liked Alexa. He knew she wasn't real, but it was fun pretending. She told him she lived in the cloud and was very happy. He was happy for her. The little things, you know.

The bird feeders we're doing fine. The bear was not tall enough to reach them, and probably wouldn't be tall enough until next year. At least Kirksey hoped so. The squirrels, or something else, we're still crapping in front of the sliding door to the deck. Kirksey had found the poop yesterday on arriving. He had done nothing then. The crap was all dry now, so Kirksey shoveled it up and threw it off the deck. He sprayed WD-40 on all the locations, hoping it would deter the practice. It had worked last year.

Diana couldn't read either. Nobody could, except the Chinese. The morning news was all spoken now. No chyrons, no graphics. That was fine, the news got out, it was just a different way to do it. The newspapers had quit publishing their print editions. They had all gone to spoken versions. They were competing head-to-head with TV for the news, and both sides knew it. Somebody would win.

In the old days, the Wall Street Journal would have opined on the topic, and Kirksey would have read it with pleasure. Of course there was no print Wall Street Journal now, but Kirksey could find its icon on his iPad. So he listened to what the Wall Street Journal had decided he should know. That was really time-consuming. Kirksey didn't do it much. You couldn't pick and choose with a linear aural stream. None of the old glorious scanning through a printed document to find what you were interested in. It was a screaming waste of time.

Kirksey's divorce mediations were going fine, at least when they got to the issues. It took a much longer time to figure out the posture of the litigation because nobody, Kirksey included, could read the pleadings that had been filed. So everyone operated from memory, and some people lied. It wasn't exactly nailing Jell-O to a wall, but sometimes it felt that way. Usually there would be a result to the mediation which satisfied both sides, even the side which had been lying. Maybe particularly the side which had been lying. But then, Kirksey thought, maybe both sides had done some lying. Kirksey reflected back on his imagined principle of Chancery court equity, "scroom." If you pronounced that, you understood the principle.

The book publishing houses were all in stasis. They didn't know what to do. They were biding their time. Audible was going great guns. That's how Kirksey got his fiction now. You could listen to any of the great literature. Dickens with his Fagin and Oliver; Homer with Ulysses; John Locke with his appropriation-by-labor; even the US Constitution and Bill of Rights. Kirksey wondered whether high school students studying the Constitution this way would retain it better than they had when they had had the luxury of printed documents in front of them.

Litigation was of course a mess. No one could file pleadings. Well, that was not quite right. You could file them if you could write them, but no one could read them, so no one filed them. What people did now was make sworn oral statements so that the litigation could proceed. Kirksey's divorce mediation practice was booming. Jello being nailed to the wall. But that was okay if the parties were happy. Kirksey was happy. He was pleasing the litigants and making a bunch of money.

Speaking of money, that was funny too. You could still read the numbers on the bills, the five or ten or twenty and so forth, you just couldn't read any of the other stuff. The stock market had taken a long time to sort out the situation. After a pause of ten days it had reopened with greatly reduced volume. All bids were spoken, and the quantities stated. Bid and ask and so forth, and it worked. But there was no computer trading because nobody could read anything on the screens except the numbers.

You could buy ten shares of Apple, but it took a long time. You called your broker and he or she got in line. Usually you got your purchase in about two weeks, and it was best to place a market order so that it would go through without a hitch. Oh, you could do limit orders and short selling and so forth if you had the patience. Kirksey didn't have the patience. He talked with Alexa about it. She said she was sorry he was sad. He told her it was okay. She said, "You bet. Have a nice day, Bill."

Kirksey talked to the bear whenever he came around. That hadn't changed. The bear didn't talk back, but then he had never talked. The bear couldn't read. At least Kirksey didn't think he could.

Driving was okay. It was fifty miles to Knoxville from Gatlinburg and Kirksey could either go by Goose Gap or the interstate. He knew what all the signs meant, even though he couldn't read them. People passing through Knoxville on I-40 and I-75 just used their nav systems, listening to the guidance. That worked just fine. People with older model cars with no nav systems were up the creek until they could buy a portable nav system.

National politics hadn't changed much. It had always been oral. Protesters didn't carry signs with writing now, but they still protested, shouting whatever was on their minds. Twitter had gone out of business. That was a blessing, Kirksey thought. There was no more cyber-bullying, another blessing. Now bullying only happened the old-fashioned way, personally. International politics hadn't changed either, except that the translators and even the sign-language people were making a lot of money.

Children didn't learn to read, but they sure learned to listen. Audible had spun off an entire Children's Division. Libraries closed. Sports continued on TV. You could read the scores, because they were all numbers. The numbers got posted next to the logo of the team. Maybe the stockbrokers would come up with logos for some of the stocks.

When he was in Gatlinburg Kirksey sometimes shot sporting clays, and that hadn't changed. You called for your birds and did your best, and the scorer marked down hit or miss with a stroke of a pencil and that was that. At the 200-yard range Kirksey used shoot-and-see targets and he had a spotting scope, so that was unchanged. The little things.

Be glad you have electricity, a bad outcome

KIRKSEY WOKE UP. IT WAS DECEMBER 19. HE DIDN'T KNOW WHAT TIME it had started, but it had been while they were sleeping. There was no electricity. Not a big deal, he thought, power failure. It will come back in a while.

But it didn't. The televisions didn't work. He thought their two iPhones would let him know what was going on. Except they didn't work either. The old transistor radio in the garage didn't work either, even with new batteries. No iphones, no radio, no TV. Kirksey and Diana did not have landlines but Kirksey thought maybe the neighbors did.

He went out and tried to talk to the neighbors. They told him to go away. But one of them did say, no, his landline did not work.

Kirksey wondered whether this whole thing might be the beginning of a physical invasion. Like that thing in *Red Storm Rising* or whatever that movie was where the Cubans landed by airplane at a school and the kids fought back.

Cars didn't work. Kirksey couldn't hear any traffic on the interstate, and he always could hear the interstate, even at night. There was no traffic on the roads near the house. He had not heard the train yet, but that was OK, because the train only came by five or six times a day. Maybe he would hear it in a while.

But by the end of the day there was still no train. It looked like most transportation had simply stopped. What about airplanes? He hadn't heard any jets, but maybe he would. There were no condensation trails in the sky.

Well, he thought, we can still travel by foot or by bicycle. Or by horse. Same as Jefferson, Adams, and George Washington. Then he started wondering where next week's supper or next month's supper would come from. How much food did they have on hand? Could he walk to Food City and get more food?

He went to Food City and found that everyone else had already thought of it. The shelves were bare, even the butcher's meat and the frozen foods.

But the toilets still flushed, the faucets still ran. The gas stove still worked. So did the barbecue grill and the fireplace gas. There was plenty of firewood split and stacked from the ash trees. Thank you, ash tree borers, for killing the trees.

It looked like the problem was only electricity. Nothing electrical worked. Did the city's water pressure depend upon electric pumps? Not all of it. That's why water tanks were up high on ridges. But some of the city's water must be pumped, right? And if so, when would the toilets stop flushing and the faucets stop running? Where would Kirksey get water? There was water in the creek behind the house. But, he thought, I will have to boil it.

And what about the natural gas lines to the stove and the grill and the fireplace? Did they depend on electricity anywhere? What pressurized the lines? Electric pumps? If so, how long do we have?

Adams, Jefferson, and Washington had lived without electricity and gas. But they had had transportation in place. Old fashioned reliable transportation. Kirksey knew there were four horses at a barn six miles down Westland Drive.

It was December 19. The only things in Kirksey's gardens now were carrots and beets. And Diana's flowers. Yes, they could eat her pansies. But the carrots and beets would not mature until late March. Could they make it until there was food from the spring and summer gardens?

It was time to start hunting squirrels and deer. Kirksey had lots of guns.

TWO WEEKS LATER

Kirksey's daughter and her husband were with them now. And their three children: six, four, and the baby of eleven months. They had walked two miles, with the baby in Aislinn's backpack and Spencer holding hands with Evvie and Weston. Some people threw rocks at them and tried to take their clothing away. Happily there were only two of them. Spencer was a big guy, so he just beat the shit out of them. Spencer walked back to their house once and found someone had broken into the house and taken everything.

Christmas was happy. They prayed and sang and counted blessings. They talked about how the baby Jesus was born without electricity and did just fine. The children looked at the baby Jesuses in the two nativity scenes Kirksey and Diana had. They said, yes, he looked happy.

Scott and Camille came by now and then. It was a dangerous trip for them, with people attacking them.

Marren and Traci and Matt had moved in with Kirksey and Diana.

They could not risk the walk.

Kirksey thought, we have our children and grandchildren with us, most of them anyway. We are blessed. Baby Jesus is happy.

All his guns were loaded. Even the old 1928 Winchester 32-20 that Fred had given him. It had belonged to Fred's grandfather, Papa Smith, who had had it in Harlan, Kentucky. Kirksey thought about his guns this way: Most of us in the house can shoot pretty well. We don't want to talk about it, about shooting someone. Then Kirksey thought about the Donner Pass. He didn't talk about the Donner Pass. Most people didn't know what happened there. Diana knew.

There were no neighborhood committees. Kirksey thought they should all be working together, parceling out food and finding shut-ins. He asked some of his neighbors. They told him to go away.

People wanted seeds, so they broke into Mayo's Garden Center. They also broke into pharmacies to get what they needed for themselves, or thought they could sell.

Kirksey thought things were going downhill fast.

FOUR WEEKS LATER

The natural gas lines were out. Kirksey had three propane tanks in Gatlinburg, but they were fifty miles away. Might as well be on the moon, he thought. There had been a dozen tanks at Ace Hardware, just five miles away. Gone now. People had just taken them.

Kirksey thought about money. He wondered, how long will we use it? He had several thousand dollars in gold and silver coins. Or that's what they had been worth on December 18, before the electromagnetic pulse, or whatever it was. Someone broke into Kirksey's house, probably to steal those coins, or whatever he could find. Kirksey shot him six times with his Smith and Wesson .38.

He then cut the man up in the backyard and smoked his flesh over the fireplace. The bones and the skull he threw in the creek for coyotes.

Water had stopped flowing a week ago. Some neighbors dug trench toilets. Some built outhouses. Kirksey loaned out a few of his hand tools and they never came back. He was glad it had only been a few.

It looked like people were no damn good, as the saying went.

Kirksey boiled creek water in the fireplace. Everyone had to boil the creek water. Kirksey was sharing his firewood, but no one thanked him. Some people had briquets and didn't need firewood.

The chickens were laying two eggs a day. They didn't have their electric coop lights which kept them laying in the winter.

SIX WEEKS LATER

Someone had taken three of the nine chickens. Kirksey wondered why they hadn't just taken them all. If he had seen it happen, he would have shot the thief. He told all the neighbors that, just in case it was one of them who had taken the chickens.

Kirksey was starting a new garden plot. Too early to plant much of anything. People wanted to borrow his gardening tools. He said no.

There was no homeschooling. Kirksey realized that with the children off the internet, parents and books could once again be repositories of knowledge. No one cared about that.

ONE YEAR LATER

Kirksey walked to the interstate a mile away. It was quiet. Grass had grown in the concrete joints. The asphalt sections were crumbling at the edges. Cars mostly sat on the shoulders, but some were in the travel lanes. There was an eighteen-wheeler where people had lived for a while. The truck's load of furniture from North Carolina had become firewood for the fire circle behind the truck. Four bodies lay on the ground, eyes pecked out by crows, and flesh torn by coyotes.

Kirksey thought about the airplanes that had fallen from the skies, no hydraulics to control the flight paths, passengers screaming.

There were no worship services at the Church of the Ascension. One neighbor said to Kirksey, "Fuck God. He allowed this to happen."

On most days the Tennessee River was unchanged. Water flowed through Loudon dam at whatever the spillway settings had been on December 18. With big rains in the mountains now, the spillway settings were inadequate and there was property damage near the river. Kirksey figured things were bad in Chattanooga. No one cared. Kirksey knew that if he asked them, they would say, "Fuck Chattanooga."

Be glad you have electricity; a good outcome

Kirksey woke up. It was December 19. He didn't know what time it had started, but it had been while they were sleeping. He woke up with no electricity. Not a big deal, he thought, power failure. It will come back in a while. But it didn't. The televisions didn't work. He thought their iPhones would let them know what was going on. Except they didn't work either. The old transistor radio out in the garage didn't work either, even with new batteries. No iphones, no radio, no TV. Kirksey and Diana did not have landlines but, Kirksey thought, maybe the neighbors did.

He went out and talked to the neighbors. Those with landlines said, no, they did not work. The neighbors thought maybe there had been some cyber event in space that had disabled the United States. They thought it might be the beginning of a physical invasion. Like that thing in *Red Storm Rising* or whatever that movie was where the Cubans landed by airplane at a school and the kids fought back. The bottom line was that everyone was guessing. Nobody knew from Shinola.

Cars didn't work. Kirksey couldn't hear any traffic on the interstate, and he always could hear the interstate, even at night. There was no traffic on the roads near the house. He had not heard the train yet, but that was OK, because the train only came by five or six times a day. Maybe he would hear it in a while.

But by the end of the day there was still no train. It looked like most transportation had simply stopped. What about airplanes? He hadn't heard any jets, but maybe he would. There were no condensation trails in the sky.

Well, he thought, we can still travel by foot or by bicycle. Or by horse. Same as Jefferson, Adams, and George Washington. Then he started wondering where next week's supper or next month's supper would come from. How much food did they have on hand? Could he walk to Food City and get more food? Yes, and he'd better do it in a hurry, before everyone else thought of it. And he thought I'd better take a gun. Just in case, he thought. I need a gun for my trip to Food City. Great. On Christmas, the day of our Lord.

But the toilets still flushed, the faucets still ran. The gas stove still worked. So did the barbecue grill and the fireplace gas. There was plenty of firewood split and stacked from the ash trees. Thank you, ash tree borers, for killing the trees.

It looked like the problem was only electricity. Nothing electrical worked. Did the city's water pressure depend upon electric pumps? Not all of it. That's why water tanks were up high on ridges. But some of the city's water must be pumped, right? And if so, when would the toilets stop flushing and the faucets stop running? Where would Kirksey get water? There was water in the creek behind the house. But, he thought, we will have to boil it.

And what about the natural gas lines to the stove and the grill and the fireplace? Did they depend on electricity anywhere? What pressurized the lines? Electric pumps? If so, how long do we have?

Adams, Jefferson, and Washington had lived without electricity and gas. But they had had transportation in place. Old fashioned reliable transportation. Kirksey knew there were four horses at a barn six miles down Westland Drive.

It was December 19. The only things in Kirksey's gardens now were carrots and beets. And Diana's flowers. Yes, they could eat her pansies. But the carrots and beets would not mature until late March. Could they make it until there was food from the spring and summer gardens?

It was time to go to Food City. And time to start hunting squirrels and deer. Kirksey had lots of guns.

TWO WEEKS LATER

Kirksey's daughter and her husband were with them now. And their three children: six, four, and the baby of eleven months. They had walked two miles, with the baby in Aislinn's backpack and Spencer holding hands with Evvie and Weston. Spencer walked back to their house every day for food, formula, and diapers. They didn't need much formula. Aislinn mostly breastfed.

Christmas was happy. They prayed and sang and counted blessings. They talked about how the baby Jesus was born without electricity and did just fine. The children looked at the baby Jesuses in the two nativity scenes Kirksey and Diana had. They said, yes, he looked happy.

Kirksey had made two trips to Food City with a backpack for groceries. Food City was running out, of course, could not resupply. But there was still lots of food in the Kirksey household, and they hadn't touched the nine chickens. The chickens were still laying eggs, but that would decline because they didn't have their lights to make it summer all the time. All the food in the freezer had thawed. Most of it had gone to the chickens, but some of it lasted outside in the shade. Natural refrigeration.

Scott and Camille checked in now and then. It was a long way for them, over three miles. Marren and Traci and Matt visited almost every day. Their walk was about a mile and a half, and Marren thought it was an adventure to walk to Abi and Papi's house. Kirksey thought every day: Diana and I have our grandchildren and children near us, most of them anyway. We are blessed. Baby Jesus is happy.

All his guns were loaded. Even the old 1928 Winchester 32-20 that Fred had given him. It had belonged to Fred's grandfather, Papa Smith, who had had it in Harlan, Kentucky. Kirksey thought about his guns this way: Most of us in the house can shoot pretty well. We don't want to talk about it, about shooting someone. Then Kirksey thought about the Donner Pass. He didn't talk about the Donner Pass. Most people didn't know what happened there. Diana knew.

Neighborhood committees were forming. They parceled out food and found shut-ins. Mayo's Garden Center and Ace Hardware were sharing seed stock, with growing instructions. Gary at Walgreens was heading a group of pharmacists collecting and guarding the prescription meds and the over-the-counter medications. Gary chaired the meetings about who got what.

Kirksey was starting to think mankind was pretty decent.

FOUR WEEKS LATER

The natural gas lines were out. Kirksey had three propane tanks in Gatlinburg, but they were fifty miles away. Might as well be on the moon, he thought. There had been a dozen propane tanks at Ace Hardware, just five miles away. Gone now.

Kirksey thought about money. He wondered, how long will we use it? He had several thousand dollars in gold and silver coins. Or that's what they had been worth on December 18, before the electromagnetic pulse, or whatever it was. But who wanted coins now? Who would give Kirksey food for them? An optimist would: "This situation can't last forever," the optimist would say. "When it is over, I will be rich."

Water had stopped flowing a week ago. Everyone in the neighborhood dug trench toilets. Then some built outhouses. Kirksey loaned out his hand tools and the tools always came back. More evidence that mankind was good. So far at least.

Kirksey boiled creek water in the fireplace. Kirksey was sharing his firewood. Everyone had to boil the creek water. Some people had briquets and didn't need firewood. The chickens were laying two eggs a day. They didn't have their electric coop lights which kept them laying in the winter.

SIX WEEKS LATER

Someone had taken three of the chickens. Kirksey wondered why they hadn't just taken them all. If he had seen it happen, would he have shot the thief? Probably. He was glad he had missed the theft. But he told all the neighbors he would have killed the thief, and then shared his flesh out with any who wanted some. Half the neighbors said, good idea, count me in.

Kirksey was helping prepare garden plots. Too early to plant much of anything.

Homeschooling had started. Some children from other neighborhoods walked in. Kirksey's neighborhood had three groups. Children three-to-six, six-to-nine, and nine-to- twelve. High schoolers helped teach. The high schoolers gathered textbooks and set up a library in the nine-to-twelve homeschool. Kirksey realized that with the children off the internet, parents and books were once again repositories of knowledge. That was good.

ONE YEAR LATER

Kirksey walked to the interstate a mile away. It was quiet. Grass had grown in the concrete joints. The asphalt sections were crumbling at the edges. Cars mostly sat on the shoulders, but some were in the travel lanes. There was an eighteen-wheeler where people had lived for a while. Its load of furniture from North Carolina had become firewood for the fire circle behind the truck. Some chairs still sat at the fire circle, not burned. Kirksey wondered where the people had gone. None of them had come to Kirksey's neighborhood.

Kirksey thought about the airplanes that must have fallen from the skies, no hydraulics to control the flight paths, passengers screaming or praying.

The Sunday and Wednesday worship services at the Church of the Ascension were packed. People needed God. The church opened a shelter for those who could not care for themselves. The church had a horse-drawn delivery cart they used to bring people in. They also toured the neighborhoods, asking for food for the shelter. People were as generous as they could be. Mankind was good, Kirksey thought.

On most days the Tennessee River was unchanged. There would be swimming in the river in the summer, Kirksey figured. And people would use their kayaks and canoes. They wouldn't be able to use their power boats. Water flowed through Loudon dam at whatever the spillway settings had been on December 18. With any big rains in the mountains now, the spillway settings were inadequate and there was property damage for homes near the river. Kirksey figured things were even worse in Chattanooga.

What if there is no fire?

Day 1

MATCHES WILL NOT LIGHT. PROPANE AND NATURAL GAS BARBECUE grills will not light. No one sits by the fireside at night and reflects upon the day. In the third world, all food is eaten raw. In the parts of the developed world which still have electricity, cooking takes place.

Day 2 into perpetuity

There are no internal combustion engines. There is no fire in the cylinders.

There are no cars, buses, or trucks, except those models which are electric. People quickly realize that the charging stations for electric vehicles get their electricity from the burning of fossil fuel, and will soon no longer function.

Municipal power plants using fossil fuel stop operating. Homeowners are left in the dark. They cannot light their candles or kerosene lamps.

Nuclear energy suddenly looks very good. Small modular reactors become the go-to option. Small modular reactors (SMRs) are advanced nuclear reactors with a power capacity of up to 300 MWe per unit, about one-third the generating capacity of traditional nuclear power reactors.

Better batteries are needed for electric vehicles. There is a worldwide shortage of lithium, and prices rise constantly.

There are no propeller planes or jet planes.

There is no balloon flight except with helium.

There is no mail delivery, no package delivery by UPS or FedEx.

Communication by radio, television, and landline telephone goes on in municipalities which have wind, battery, and solar backup power.

Smartphone email is unaffected because Apple and Samsung have wind, battery, and solar backup.

Bicycle sales are robust. Trek, Schwinn, and Raleigh stock prices rise. Skateboarding grows. Where there is snow, people use trekking skis and poles.

Day 3

Homeowners with gas water heaters take cold showers. Hotels and motels with gas water heaters refund 50% of lodgers' booking costs. Homeowners are urged by radio and television to remove car batteries and use that power source for home lighting with LED bulbs.

Day 4

Travelocity and Expedia book only electrically-heated lodgings.

Day 5

Because there are no internal combustion cars, buses, or trucks, and also no diesel engines for trains, and no engines at all for river shipping, huge supply chain problems appear. Stores sell out of inventory. There is hoarding. Sailboats could be used for river shipping, but how to get the goods to the piers?

Day 6

There are no functioning barbecue pits.

Day 7

The US Atomic Energy Agency streamlines the permitting process for new nuclear plants. Urges use of SMRs.

Day 8

All developed countries ramp up helium production.

Day 10

Chefs hate cooking without gas, and search for the best electric stoves. Martha Stewart suggests particular models, and adapts some of her recipes to electricity. She concedes that omelets are difficult with electric cooktops.

Ree Drummond cancels her "Prairie Woman" cooking shows.

Day 50

Homeowners wonder what to do with their non-functioning fireplaces. Some convert them into storage cabinets.

Day 60

"Memphis in May," an annual barbecue celebration, is canceled.

Day 62

"The Rendezvous" and thirty other Memphis barbecue restaurants consider going out of business, but begin experimenting with electrically cooked beef, pork, and ribs. They use artificial smoke flavors. The product is underwhelming. Additionally, there is no tourist clientele, only walk-ins and cyclists. All but three restaurants close.

Day 70

US and European fire hose manufacturers join buggy-whip makers on the ash heap of irrelevance.

Day 100

Black-backed woodpeckers lack their preferred habitat of burned forest. Their numbers decline but the birds do not become extinct.

Day 105 into perpetuity

Forests just grow and grow, and never burn. Lightning formerly produced fires on the ground, but it does not do so now. Wind blows down hyper-tall trees.

Those few fire departments which have electric vehicles use those vehicles only for emergency response. All departments respond locally to emergencies with bicycles. Most firefighters find other jobs.

What if all the TVA dams vanished?

Day 1

CHAOS AND FLOODING. 614 DEATHS. PROPERTY DAMAGE. THE FORT Loudoun Reservoir is gone. It had been the uppermost in a chain of nine TVA reservoirs making a navigable 652-mile channel from Knoxville to Paducah, Kentucky.

Day 2

Because Loudoun Dam and Tellico Dam are gone, The Little Tennessee river exists once again. Formerly it was a premier trout fishing stream. Now it is back, but it has no trout. It also has no snail darters.

Day 9

Letters to the editor suggest that China is behind the disappearance of the dams. No explanation of how China could have done such a thing is put forward.

Day 12

Editorials debunk the China theory, pointing out that China is a centrally planned economy and would be unlikely to cast discredit on President Roosevelt, also a central planner.

Day 15

Because there is now no river shipping for those 652 miles, trucking, air freight, and rail shipping increase. Stock prices of FedEx and Norfolk Southern rise. The United States Postal Service hires new workers in Tennessee, Alabama, and Kentucky.

Day 20

Homes, cottages, docks, and all other waterfront facilities sit high and dry. Property values plummet. Mortgage companies file bankruptcies.

Day 21

A billion-dollar tourist industry associated with boating, fishing, and water skiing collapses. Ancillary businesses and jobs are eliminated. This has a severe impact on local economies.

The University of Tennessee rowing team now lacks flat water for training. The university disbands the team, searches for a new women's sport to avert Title IX troubles.

Day 25

Interest in the snail darter rises. The TVA power grid fails due to the lack of hydroelectric power.Wind and solar supply scant intermittent power. Homes, businesses, hospitals, churches, elder care facilities have no power. There are no lights, air conditioning, or heating. Electrical appliances do not work. Flights are cancelled due to lack of instrument landing systems and runway lighting. Airports are dark and have no communications. People and cargo are stranded. The trout in the Clinch and Holston rivers die due to the lack of cold water.

People wonder why the Tellico Dam was ever built. They learn that University of Tennessee professor David Etnier discovered the snail darter in The Little Tennessee in 1973. They also learn that under the National Environmental Policy Act, lawsuits were filed because the Tellico Reservoir to be created would alter the habitat of the river and kill the endangered snail darter.

They learn that the NEPA lawsuits slowed but did not stop the Tellico Dam. They also learn that even though the Supreme Court upheld NEPA protection, Congress specifically exempted the snail darter from that protection. They learn that after the Tellico Dam and its reservoir were completed in 1979, the snail darter was wiped out in the Little Tennessee.

Day 30

Insurance companies deny all property damage and death claims, calling the disappearance of the TVA dams an "act of God."

Day 40

The Tennessee Trial Lawyers Association files a class action lawsuit against the insurance companies.

Day 50

The TTLA amends its lawsuit to add TVA as a defendant. The landowners on what had been Melton Hill Lake join the class action lawsuit, their formerly lakefront property now being high and dry.

Day 55

TVA hires five new lawyers for its General Counsel's office. Because courts are closed due to no electricity, the five new TVA lawyers are fired.

Day 56

The limited intermittent power from wind and solar is extremely expensive. When it is available, so many buyers chase it, the price jumps.

Day 57

Citizens and police cannot communicate. Crime soars. The streets are dark. Businesses, shops, stores, and homes are looted. People search for food and water. No water has flowed to homes from the moment electricity to pump it disappeared. Chaos reigns.

Day 80

Spring floods return. Farms, residences, businesses, roads, and bridges are destroyed.

Day 100

Trout from Abrams Creek in the Great Smoky Mountains National Park spread downstream and begin to populate The Little Tennessee. Sales of fly fishing gear rise at Bass Pro, LL Bean, Three Rivers Anglers, and Orvis.

What if the NFL introduces flexible field length?

Week 1

THE NFL TELLS FRANCHISE OWNERS THEY MAY USE PLAYING FIELDS (ON their home fields) 80 yards long, 140 yards long, or simply stay with the conventional 100-yard fields. All other rules are to remain unchanged.

The additional forty-yard area is to be located in the middle of the field between two 50-yard lines. The area is to be marked with multiple Xs, and is to be called the "X area."

Week 2

Teams with losing records decide to change to one of the new lengths for their home fields. Teams with winning records stay with conventional length.

Week 3

On the 80-yard fields, kickoffs from the 35-yard line uniformly produce touchbacks, and the ball is placed on the 25-yard line.

Because the field is shorter, teams with excellent punters have an easier time putting the receiving team in bad field position.

On the 140-yard fields, kickoffs from the 35-yard line travel about 70 yards, to the other 35-yard line. Because the kicking team has to run those 70 yards, the receiving player has time to attempt a runback rather than fair-catching the ball. Fans like the change.

Week 16

Noting that the USFL and XFL have once again come into existence, the NFL owners decide to further increase their own fan interest.

They reach an agreement with the two inferior leagues that at the end of those leagues' seasons, the top USFL and XFL teams will play each other. The winner of that game will then play against the NFL team with the worst record. If the USFL or XFL team wins, the NFL team is demoted to the league that beat them, and the USFL/XFL team gets a season to prove itself in the NFL.

The USFL and XFL are delighted to have a chance at the big show, and so are the fans.

Teleporting by sight

Day 1

KIRKSEY DIDN'T KNOW HOW IT WORKED, BUT IT HAD STARTED WITH children playing soccer. When a child needed to be at a place where she wasn't, she simply thought herself to the place on the field she needed to be. Soon all the children on the field were doing it. The parents didn't understand what was going on, but they could see it.

Day 7

The parents couldn't do it at first, but in the next week the children had taught them. You could teleport yourself to any place you could see. But you had to be able to see it.

Day 8

Some of the soccer parents were in the Army Reserve. They immediately saw military possibilities. Before long, the Chinese Communist Party learned what was going on in Tennessee. They knew, they just knew, that this was a clever military plot aimed against them.

But it turned out that you could only teleport with what you could hold in your hands or carry on your back. Not both. So for military purposes it was limited to rapid movements of a few soldiers. But it was good for that.

Day 50

Later that summer there were some mistakes. You could see the moon. But if you teleported yourself there without thinking, "There's no air up there," well, you didn't come back.

Kirksey wondered whether it would be possible to put on a space suit, teleport yourself to the moon, and look back to the Earth, and come home. He didn't know. He wasn't going to try.

Day 365

On clear days, Kirksey would teleport himself to Mount LeConte. From there he would teleport in stages to the Clingman's Dome parking lot. He would then walk the last half mile to the Clingman's Dome tower, from the top of which he could see West Knoxville. Then he would teleport home.

Teleporting by coordinates

Day 1

WORLDWIDE COMMUTING IS POSSIBLE, SO LONG AS THE PERSON teleporting has the exact latitude and longitude of the destination. The method is much more user-friendly than teleporting by sight, which was the only teleportation that had existed for many years.

Once again, the traveler is limited to what he can carry in his hands and in a pack on his back. Teleportation cannot be used to arrive inside a structure. If coordinates are attempted which would achieve that, the teleportation simply fails.

However, teleportation is excellent for escaping after committing a robbery or a break-in.

Day 4

Television reporting of teleporters escaping after robberies and break-ins causes an increase in handgun sales in the US. Canadians and Europeans clamor for a change in their gun laws.

Day 5

Because teleporting travelers can't transport much, there is still a need for air freight, shipping, trucking, and rail transportation. But airlines, having lost most passenger traffic, lose value on stock markets worldwide. Some airline passengers wanting to travel with more than they can carry still fly in the traditional way, but those travelers are few.

Day 34

Hartmann, American Tourister, Briggs & Riley, Eagle Creek, and Delsey bring out stylish, comfortable backpacks.

Day 45

Adultery is much easier now.

Day 110

Canada refuses to change its gun laws. Britain allows its citizens to carry guns.

Day 180

Adultery does not always go undiscovered. Divorces increase. Lawyers' caseloads rise. Marriages decrease.

Kirksey wondered about geese

EIGHT GEESE HAD JUST FLOWN OVER KIRKSEY AT LAKESHORE PARK. HE wondered whether they defecated from the air.

When he got home, Kirksey went to the internet and found out that any bird can poop wherever it is: sitting, flying, walking around.

But, he said to himself, goose turds on the ground look like shortish green cigarettes. They are solid.

Kirksey wondered whether those cigarettes would fall from the sky. The internet insisted that all bird defecation was liquid, being a mixture of urine and poop, and all delivered out one hole, the cloaca.

But geese? What about those green cigarettes? They weren't liquid. Kirksey feared airborne geese, having only the solid form available to them, well, would just let fly from the air. He didn't know. He was worried.

Kirksey saw "Bibles 20% off"

IT WAS A SIGN IN THE WINDOW OF A CHRISTIAN BOOKSTORE. He wondered if those bibles had all the words. If not, which 20% had been cut? What part of the bible did someone think was expendable?

Certainly not the creation stories, even though they could do with some reconciling. Certainly not the four gospels, nor Acts, nor the Pauline letters. So, maybe it was some of the arcane stuff in the Old Testament. Maybe that was the place.

Kirksey wondered whether there had been a commission to make the decisions, as there had been when the King James version came into being. He hoped so.

Be glad you can smell and taste

KIRKSEY KNEW THAT THERE WAS A DIFFERENCE BETWEEN SMELL AND taste. Smell was in the nose and taste was in the mouth. He'd gotten up that morning and brewed his tea, added milk to it, and put it in the microwave. A normal day in Gatlinburg in the big house. He put some raisin cinnamon bread in the toaster and took a sip of the tea. It had no flavor. That's odd, he thought. Well, he'd worked hard yesterday. Maybe it was just a symptom of tiredness.

He could not smell the bread toasting. When the toaster was done Kirksey took the slices out, stacked them up, and cut them into fourths. They had no flavor. More tiredness, he thought. He ate a piece of ham. No flavor there either. Oh well, it was an odd morning.

He called Diana. They talked about the hummingbird at the Gatlinburg feeder. She said she had one in Knoxville. Kirksey told her he had a busy little wren who was making a racket pecking the hot cranberry seed cakes. They were about finished talking when Kirksey asked, how do things taste to you this morning? Why do you ask? she asked. Because oh, I don't know, I don't taste anything this morning. It's not, he said, how it was with Effie, that when she got older things didn't taste right. Effie only meant that things didn't taste the way she remembered them. Yes, Diana said, I remember you telling me that about her. I wish I had known your grandmother. Well, Kirksey said, call me back after breakfast and tell me how things are going.

Diana called back. It's weird, she said. I can't taste anything either. Have you turned on the news? Kirksey asked. No, she said. Well, when you do, he said, let me know if they have anything. That afternoon she called. Evidently the talking heads on TV couldn't taste anything either. Was it the Chinese again?

THIRTY DAYS LATER

There was a new product on the market called Eat This!. Of course it had no flavor. Nothing had any flavor, but Eat This! made noise when you chewed it, and you could feel it in your mouth. Noise and feel were the big things for food these days. Eat This! was loaded with nutrition. Four slices gave you all an adult needed per day.

The pizza chains we're taking it in the rear. Nobody could justify the price for something they couldn't taste, even though it looked good and felt pretty good in the mouth. Papa John's was hurting, Domino's too, all of them.

But Eat This! was doing very well. It came in various colors. There was also a squishy version of Eat This! which you could wipe into the grooves of celery stalks, to get something that made noise you could feel in your mouth. Kirksey hadn't tried that yet. But he had several boxes of regular Eat This!. Maybe he would get the squishy stuff.

The grocery stores were hurting. They had always operated on a thin margin, and now that was gone. No one was buying much in the way of fresh vegetables and certainly not steaks and pork chops or wild-caught salmon. The economy of the US was in trouble. The stock market was adjusting, as it always did, building the new strangeness into its projections for profitability. The mutual funds were adjusting.

The usual conspiracy geeks were out there on Twitter, blaming the Chinese, or blaming Isis, or blaming the Republicans, or blaming Donald Trump. Kirksey thought that blaming someone for something had become the new background noise of American political life

The talking heads on TV talked about the difference between taste and smell. They spent a lot of time on it. With the need to fill the twenty-four hour news cycle, they had to talk about something. It wasn't as simple as Kirksey had thought, just nose versus mouth. It turned out that taste and smell had their own receptor organs. Chemicals in foods were detected by taste buds, special sensory cells. When stimulated, those cells sent signals to specific areas of the brain, giving the perception of taste. And specialized cells in the nose picked up airborne odor molecules. The odor molecules stimulated receptor proteins on cilia at the tips of sensory cells, initiating a neural response.

Kirksey learned that taste distinguished chemicals with a sweet, salty, sour, bitter, or umami taste. Five tastes. Umami, Kirksey learned, was Japanese for "savory." Taste and smell were separate activities. Well, big deal, Kirksey thought. They are both gone. Time for an Eat This! cracker.

What if no planes and helicopters?

Day 1

THERE ARE NO CONTRAILS IN THE SKY. THERE IS NO CONDENSATION OF water from jet fuel combustion.

Day 50

People have turned to lighter-than-air flight, using balloons. Hydrogen is avoided, because of the 1937 Hindenburg disaster. (Germany had designed the Hindenburg to use helium, but could not get it because the USA had embargoed it. So the Germans used hydrogen instead.)

Day 51

Although some balloons used helium from day 50 onward, most balloons use hot air produced by tanks of propane or natural gas. Directional travel is possible by external fans mounted on the balloons, as was done with the Hindenburg.

Day 75

Airlines worldwide are bankrupt. Their stock values plummet to cents per share.

Day 100

FedEx Air closes its doors, finding balloon transport of goods too costly. FedEx Ground expands.

Day 110

The US Postal Service has eliminated air mail.

Day 115

People use email and text messaging for their mail. Sales of home computers and iphones rise.

What if everything is perfect?

No one needs anything beyond what he already has. Everyone is efficient and kind. No one takes advantage of anyone else. There is no point in it.

When there is nothing efficient and kind to do, people stand in one place and go to sleep.

Everyone is happy.

What if text message reminders escape control?

Day 1

ALL TEXT MESSAGE REMINDERS FROM DOCTORS' OFFICES, DENTAL offices, dermatology offices, lawn services, retail stores--in short, all computer generated reminders--simply do not go out. They disappear.

Day 2

However, the next day new messages go out to all the then-intended recipients of Day 1 messages. These messages pull content randomly from the Day 1 messages. So, for example, Luella Blake receives a message that she has an appointment on Day 3 with Dr. Norman Kirk.

This confuses Luella and she calls Dr. Kirk's office. Dr. Kirk's receptionist tells Luella, no, she has no appointment, but would she like to make one? Luella declines.

Such messages churn out all through the United States and Canada.

Day 3

The next day, the medical reports intended for all the Day 1 persons are put in a hat, so to speak, shaken up, and then sent to any Day 1 person whatsoever. This causes great consternation: Joe Hawthorne is told his liver blood analysis is abnormal.

Day 4

Apple and Samsung try but fail to safeguard their text messages.

Day 5

Confusion reigns in Canada for subscribers to Rogers, Bell Telus, Freedom Mobile, Sasktel, and Quebecor.

Day 6

The Day 1 persons who really did want to send messages realize that they must speak personally to their customers. They commence live calls, answering questions, and reassuring the customers that, yes, this really is Dr. Kirk's office calling.

Day 10

New office staff is needed to make these live calls. This of course increases the costs of the callers' offices in the US and Canada. The extra cost is passed on to customers through higher charges.

Day 16

A class action suit is filed under Rule 23 of the Federal Rules of Civil Procedure against AT&T, Verizon, US Cellular, T-Mobile, Visible, Metro by T-Mobile, Google Fi, Mint Mobile, Xfinity Mobile, Boost Mobile, Consumer Cellular, and Cricket Wireless. The class action is duly certified and class counsel is appointed under FRCP 23(g).

Day 45

A settlement is proposed under FRCP 23(e) that all persons who paid, or may yet have to pay, these higher charges receive a lump sum award of $5000 regardless of how long such higher charges continue. Defendants admit no liability, terming the payments "demonstrations of corporate goodwill." Class counsel accepts the settlement. The court accepts the settlement.

What if all data is known by all?

THERE IS NO DEBATE ABOUT FACTS OR ANALYSIS OF DATA. NUMBERS and statistics speak for themselves, and are known to be sufficient. All policy is based solely on probabilities and rational behavior. All decisions are probability-weighted in terms of risk and reward.

If an infectious virus appears, no one objects to taking the recommended vaccine for protection, because the chance of a side effect from that vaccine is infinitesimal. It makes more statistical sense to take the vaccine.

Society becomes more risk-tolerant. It has less fear of small probabilities, because it knows the chances of bad consequences are tiny.

What if all people look the same?

<u>Day 1</u>

IT WAS A SHOCK. BUT THERE WERE MALE AND FEMALE VERSIONS. Family members knew each other. Children duplicated their adults, they were just smaller than their adults.

<u>Day 7</u>

People realize that they have different personalities and physical abilities. Not everyone can rock climb or run fast. People have different voices. They speak different languages.

<u>Day 30</u>

People realize there are no longer recognizable ethnicities. No Chinese, no American Indians, no Negroes, no Hawaiians. Discrimination becomes impossible.

<u>Six months later</u>

The United Negro College Fund closes its doors. The ACLU loses most of its funding.

Arabs, Israelis, and Palestinians all look alike, so there is no conflict in the Middle East. No one can tell who it was he formerly hated, and no one tells which group he formerly belonged to.

Russians and Ukrainians cannot recognize each other. The Crimean region becomes peaceful. Again, no self-disclosure.

The Chinese cannot identify Uyghrs to persecute. And the Uyghrs wisely do not engage in practices which would identify them.

Seven months later

Some people have died. People learn that they indeed will die after a normal lifespan.

Nine months later

Photos are removed from all passports. Passports still exist, but they are based on fingerprints.

Shoplifting blossoms. No one can be prosecuted unless fingerprints are found on the stolen items. All shoplifters begin wearing gloves.

Home invasions become popular. People increase gun purchases, buy guns, get carry permits, and shoot invaders. Because invaders can be fingerprinted whether dead or alive, it can be determined whether there is a connection to the invaded premises. If the invaders are alive after being shot, they are prosecuted and convicted.

NRA membership increases.

Lawyers expand their criminal caseloads.

What if we cannot walk?

<u>Year 1:</u>

It is clear that the problem came from China, another product of gain-of-function research at Wuhan.

China immediately offers walkers at bargain prices. They are ready to fill the sudden need of the entire world.

Mobile scooters are in high demand. The prices of scooter firms listed on stock exchanges skyrocket.

People buy braces for their withered legs, so that their legs can bear weight. People totter about. It is sloppy, but they are walking. Because of the braces, sales of crutches increase.

People gain weight from want of exercise. Diabetes increases.

<u>Year 2:</u>

People only need one or two pairs of shoes, so shoe companies consolidate, fold, or go bankrupt. Soon there are only two shoe companies left in the US. That is fine for the two surviving companies, but not good for the stocks of the other companies, or the mutual funds which had held them. Some brokers lose their jobs.

The cheap Chinese walkers are great. People buy them, even though the Chinese are resented for causing the disease. The basic principle of capitalism triumphs: If it is a bargain, buy it.

What if no one dies?

IMMORTALITY. NO AGING. EVERYONE DEVELOPS TO MAXIMUM HEIGHT, and then lives on. Accidental death is still possible, and does occur, but death of natural causes is gone. Suicide remains possible.

There is no cancer. There is also no diabetes, not even the USA's favorite affliction, voluntary diabetes brought on by obesity. Now people just get fat with no disease.

Year 5:

Doctors go out of business because there is nothing to treat. The American Medical Association disbands.

Suicides increase in response to boredom. Psychologists propose that uncertainty is necessary to a healthy life. The American Psychological Association membership grows, picking up many doctors from the disbanded AMA.

Lawyers prosper, being able to inject uncertainty into everything. The American Bar Association increases its dues. Lawyers pay the increased dues. Law schools increase enrollment.

People remember Tennyson's poem *Tithonus*:

> The woods decay, the woods decay and fall,
> The vapors weep their burthen to the ground,
> Man comes and tills the field and lies beneath,
> And after many a summer dies the swan.
> Me only cruel immortality
> Consumes: I wither slowly in thine arms . . .

Year 10:

There is overpopulation. People worry about it, but there is no problem yet. The US is able to sell all its grain. Farmers are happy.

Year 500:

There has been a food shortage for many years. People are hungry, and getting thinner. But no one dies.

The colonies on the moon and mars have expanded to maximum capacity. There is no faster-than-light travel, despite being popular in science fiction. The population of the earth, moon, and mars is stuck. There is no more room.

Landlords have charged maximum rents for decades. The stock markets have collapsed because no one believes there will be a livable future.

The boredom-induced suicides which appeared in year two increase modestly.

The Malthus Society grows. It encourages members to commit suicide as soon as possible, but especially on February 13, to mark the birthday of Thomas Robert Malthus.

Some people do, which helps the overpopulation slightly.

The basic dilemma remains.

Year 600:

Thought turns again to faster-than-light travel. Astronomers have long known of many possibly habitable planetary systems. NASA gets a budget increase.

What if there is no money?

Day 1

THERE IS NO FIAT CURRENCY, THAT IS, NO INTRINSICALLY WORTHLESS paper "backed by the full faith and credit of the U.S. government." And no fiat currency in developed nations. Without money, there are no placeholders for transactions.

Day 2

There are of course gold non-government coins and gold bullion. There are silver non-government coins and silver bullion. People use these to purchase goods, and to assist in barter.

Day 3

People quickly realize their principal needs are food, shelter, clothing, and the affirmation of others. Mutual help becomes extremely important.

Day 4

In the third world, money was always used less than barter, so the total disappearance of money is less of an aggravation here than elsewhere.

But the developed world's trading systems collapse. Stock markets close. Mutual funds cease all transactions. National and international trade stop. Shipping by air, water, truck, and rail stop. Shipments en route when money disappears arrive at their destinations and are abandoned, there being no way to pay for them. These are then stolen.

Day 6

Charities urge donation of things instead of money.

Day 30

Turbotax updates itself to deal with a non-currency world.

Day 40

Church attendance increases. Millennialists see the disappearance of money as the beginning of the end of times. Atheists see the disappearance of money as proof that there is no God.

Day 70

Enrollment in theological schools rises.

What if there is no telephone?

Day 1

THERE IS NO CALLING UP FRIENDS OR GRANDMA.

Day 5

Because the internet still exists, communication occurs electronically, impersonally.

Day 30

Bars increase business. People need personal conversations. Drop-ins on neighbors rise. Teatime is reborn.

What if no friction between solid objects?

THERE IS GRAVITY BUT NO FRICTION. CARS STAY ON THE SURFACE OF the earth because there is gravity, but the cars cannot move. The wheels do not grab.

Trains and trucks cannot move. Shipping is unaffected, because water is not solid.

Society adapts to the problems on land by using opposing magnets and tiny jet thrusters. The thrusters work because there is still some friction in the air.

What if the tooth fairy . . .

Do you think the Tooth Fairy has always been the way she is now? With a pretty dress, pink wings, and a crown on her head? Well, let me tell you, the first tooth fairy was a man, and he is the real, honest-to-goodness tooth fairy! The Tooth Fairy you know about, the pretty lady, actually just helps him.

The Tooth Fairy, the real tooth fairy, is a great big, sloppy man. He has wide shoulders and a bulging stomach. His shirt tails hang out. Sometimes his shoes aren't tied. His hands are dirty all the way up to his elbows. His pockets are full of nuts, bolts, spark plugs, not quite finished sandwiches, marbles, pictures of his dog, and two or three shoelaces.

I met him at the post office. I was mailing a letter. A big man with greasy arms was wrapping a package using pink chewing gum to stick the flaps down.

"Don't use chewing gum," I said. "Use string."

He looked at me and sighed. "I would if I had any," said the man. He took some more chewing gum out of his mouth and stuck down another flap. "I used up all my string and all my extra shoelaces on the first package. I usually carry extra shoelaces."

I asked him why he carried extra shoe laces. He said, "You never can tell when you are going to lose a shoelace." I thought that made sense. "Especially when you don't keep them tied," he said.

That made sense too, in a way. Then he said, "And shoelaces are useful for tying up packages if you don't have a string. Do you have any extra shoe laces?"

"Well," I said, "I do have two shoelaces."

"You mean the ones in your shoes?"

"Yes."

"You'd let me use them?"

"I suppose," I said.

He smiled. "I really appreciate this. You can call me TF, if you want."

That's how I met him. After he mailed his package, we went to get a milkshake and he told me he was the Tooth Fairy.

"No, you're not," I said. "You can't be the Tooth Fairy. The Tooth Fairy is delicate and clean, and swoops down waving a wand."

"Oh," he said. "You mean Wanda Jean. She is my helper."

And so I learned the whole story. I learned that he always lands with a clump and a clutter, and leaves a mess behind him when he flies off. He told me that's one of the reasons he wasn't actively in the fairy business any more. He wasn't really suited for it. He said he was such a bad tooth fairy that he almost got fired.

But he had figured out how to get the job done without having to do it himself.

When TF first started, he could get all his deliveries done every night. He would fly to the house of each child who had lost a tooth that day, flutter in at the window, take the child's tooth from under the pillow, and put a dime in its place. The child would wake up the next morning, find the dime, and know that the Tooth Fairy had been there.

Things went that way for quite a while. No problems. Then TF began to land at all-night restaurants for a snack. At first it was only now and then, and only for a piece of pie. After a while he stopped every night for a milkshake, and a sandwich, and a piece of pie. Soon he stopped several times a night. He gained a lot of weight. And on those nights he didn't get all his deliveries done. Half the children who'd lost teeth the day before would wake up with no dimes.

This was not good. The Tooth Fairy got into trouble with his boss, the Head Fairy.

Probably the second reason the Tooth Fairy had a hard time getting all his deliveries done was his car. Now you might think that the car would help for deliveries, but it didn't. You see, flying is a much better way to get the dimes delivered.

But TF liked his car. It was old, with a silver bird on the hood. TF sometimes thought it was a bird, and sometimes he thought it was a special kind of fairy with a funny head. He called the bird Pontiac, because that was the word underneath it. His car had dents, and scratched places, smooth tires, and seat covers which were all soft and torn from lots of sitting. TF changed the backrest on the driver side so he would have room for his wings.

Being a Tooth Fairy is a year-round job, he said, a harder job than the one Santa Claus has. Children lose teeth every day and he couldn't go out in a sleigh one night and then go back home and rest.

TF's car had only one headlight and wouldn't go into second gear. So he had to go fast in first gear, and then shift into third. The horn went Booga! Booga! Booga! The turn signals didn't work. That didn't bother TF. When he needed to turn he would just crank down the window and stick out a wing to point where he was going.

The car broke down a lot. TF carried tools and spare parts with him. That led to special problems.

Sometimes instead of a dime, TF would leave a greasy spark plug under a pillow. Then when the child woke up in the morning, he would see his tooth was gone and he would know that somebody had been there. He wouldn't know who had been there, or what to do with the greasy spark plug. The tooth fairy thought a spark plug was a special gift.

Instead of a dime or a spark plug, sometimes the Tooth Fairy would leave a piece of a sandwich. He thought that was much better than a dime. Once he left a tomato from his garden. It had been a nice ripe tomato. But in the morning after a boy had slept on it all night it was more like ketchup.

It wasn't long before the head Fairy called TF in, and said that he was going to put a warning in his file. The Tooth Fairy said he would try harder to do everything right, but things didn't really change.

TF got more and more warnings in his files. Some nights he wouldn't even come close to finishing his route, so he would have to work extra hard the next night to finish a route and a half.

TF got most behind when children woke up. He would stay and talk with them. And then he would take them riding up and down the highway in his car, blowing the horn Booga! Booga! Booga! and playing the radio. One night he took four children to a drive-in restaurant where they all had chocolate milkshakes. TF had three chocolate milkshakes all by himself. The next morning, when the children woke up, the teeth they had put under their pillows were gone, and in their place were chocolate milkshake straws. The children were very happy, but their mothers and daddies were confused.

All this got to be too much for the head Fairy. He called TF in and said, "Look, Tooth Fairy, you have 80 warnings and 43 complaints in your file. I think your attitude is poor"

"HF, I . . ."

"Last night you went out on your route and you only got to half the children."

"I know, HF. I couldn't remember the others."

"Couldn't remember! Didn't you write down their names and addresses?"

"No. I can usually remember them all."

"My, my," said the Head Fairy. "This won't do. From now on, write all the names down."

"Yes, HF."

So the Tooth Fairy did just that. He wrote down all the names and addresses, and he tried to figure out the best way to go from one house to another, and whether to take his car or not. But his handwriting was so sloppy that sometimes he couldn't read what he had written. And the paper would get greasy from the spark plugs. So all in all, things didn't get much better.

The Head Fairy found out about this and decided to send a Secretary Fairy. She was little, had pink wings, and wore a crown on her head. She was very organized, and her arms were clean. She wrote out the addresses in neat handwriting.

For a while everything was fine. TF could read the list, and he could get to the places in time. He did a very good job for about six weeks. Then he started spending his extra time at drive-in restaurants with carloads of children, and riding up and down the highway, leaving the wrong things under pillows.

The Head Fairy called him in for another conference. "Tooth Fairy," he said, "you've got the easiest job in the whole fairy operation. I'm going to shift you to another division. How about dancing around toadstools?"

"But, HF . . ."

"Nothing hard," said the Head Fairy. "A basic two-step is good enough . . ."

"Boss, delivering dimes isn't easy. There are just lots of children, and they are all losing teeth. It would help if we could get the children organized, you know, so the same number would lose teeth each day.

Some nights I have a list so long that I couldn't make it with a jet plane. Also, the dimes are heavy. I've got to carry these sacks of dimes and fly at the same time. Have you ever tried that? Let me tell you, it's not easy. That is why I got the car."

"The car is no good," said the head Fairy. "It slows you down. Besides, it gets you greasy and you are getting the pillow slips dirty. Also, you need to tuck in your shirt."

The Tooth Fairy tucked in his shirt. "Listen Boss," said TF, "I've got an idea. Instead of delivering the dimes, why don't we just mail them out?"

"No," said the Head Fairy, "that won't do. There is a tradition to remember. We've always delivered the dimes, and we're going to keep delivering them."

"Listen, Boss," said TF, "I flap around all night carrying heavy sacks of dimes. Sometimes the windows are locked, and I have to come in by the door. Sometimes the door is locked, and I have to come down the chimney. Then the children wake up and talk to me and that slows me down, but I like it. Sometimes dogs bark at me. Guys who are working the night shift point at my wings and laugh. This job is not a piece of cake."

"Cake. I'm glad you said that," said the Head Fairy. "I've got a complaint right here . . . Let's see, Bobby Miller, 4312 Stonington Drive, woke up this morning with what used to be chocolate cake under his pillow. It was a big brown mess. Did you do that?"

"Yes, I was out of dimes. A whole sack of them fell in a river, so I left him a piece of chocolate cake from my lunch."

"It was a mess."

"Maybe I should have wrapped it up," said TF.

"This is your last chance," said the Head Fairy. "Get out there in distribution and do a good job."

Well, TF had an idea. That night he went out on his route and he took the Secretary Fairy with him. He gave Wanda Jean all the easy jobs to do and she did them perfectly. They got the route finished at about four in the morning and went home early.

The next night he gave Wanda Jean more of the addresses, and the next night even more, and each time she did a perfect job and got done early. In fact she did such a good job, and liked it so much, that in a week TF let her do the whole route one night. She got back at three in the morning, the route all finished, all the dimes delivered, and made him a cup of hot chocolate, with two slices of cinnamon toast.

The Tooth Fairy knew a good thing when he saw it. He asked her if she would like to do the route every night and she said, oh yes, she certainly would. TF explained that this was highly irregular and that they would have to keep their arrangement a secret. Wanda Jean said that was fine with her. She liked the work.

TF said that he would help her whenever she wanted, and that she could count on him to do the deliveries close by the distribution center. He would use his car. And, he said, every night when she got back they would have cinnamon toast and hot chocolate, and he would read her a story. On Saturdays he would even let her help him tune his car.

Wanda Jean thought that this was a fine arrangement. And that is how they have been working it ever since. The Tooth Fairy stays home, plays with his dog, reads books, and works on his car. He makes a few deliveries around the distribution center. Then Wanda Jean comes home from doing the real work, and he fixes her hot chocolate and cinnamon toast and he reads her a story. They are happy, the Head Fairy is happy, and best of all, the dimes get delivered every night.

So, the next time you are at the post office, look around to see if there is a big, sloppy man wrapping a package. It may be the Tooth Fairy and you can loan him your shoelaces. I did.

What if there is no religion?

THERE IS NO RECOURSE TO A HIGHER POWER. PEOPLE ARE ON THEIR own, bereft of comfort. There is no Christ, no Buddah, no Allah, and never have been.

Where there were houses of worship, they are repurposed for commerce. The same happens to theology school buildings.

What if speech is unintelligible?

IT SOUNDS FINE TO THE SPEAKER, WHO HEARS IT IN HIS HEAD. BUT THE person spoken to cannot understand what was said. The listener hears the sounds, but they mean nothing to him.

Radio ceases to exist in most places, or the stations simply broadcast music.

Television turns to closed captioning to set out what the speakers are saying. The same is in operas and stage plays, with closed captioning projected in the theaters.

What if there is ESP?

IT IS SAID THERE ARE SIX FORMS OF EXTRASENSORY PERCEPTION.

1. The first is telepathy, the ability to know another person's thoughts. A telepath communicates with another person by using only their mind. Of all the types of extrasensory perception, telepathy is the most researched.

2. The second is precognition, the ability to see into the future. Precognition comes from two Latin words meaning before and knowing.

3. The third is retrocognition, the ability to see into the past; oftentimes, the distant past. Persons with this perception can recognize people, places, and events of the past, even ones they had nothing to do with. Many associate this type of ESP with the phenomenon of déjà vu. Persons with retrocognition are sometimes used in investigative cases. The word comes from two Latin words meaning behind and knowing.

4. The fourth is telekinesis, the ability to have an effect on another object without any physical energy. The word "psychokinesis" comes from two Greek words meaning mind and movement.

5. The fourth is clairvoyance, the ability to see information about an object, person, scenario, location, or event (past, present, or future). It is generally strongest during practiced meditation. The term comes from two French words meaning clear and seeing.

6. The sixth and last is mediumship, the supposed ability to communicate with the dead.

Kirksey saw a sign reading "Knoxville Lice Clinic"

It was in front of a small building on Sutherland Avenue. There were solo law firms and Ph.D. counseling psychologists on the same street.

Kirksey thought it was nice that the lice had a place to go to when they were sick.

They probably didn't have primary care providers. And they probably didn't even have insurance.

So that meant if they needed emergency care, they would have to go to the University of Tennessee emergency room. Which they could not do, because they couldn't drive.

So the lice had better hope they never needed emergency care.

What if oxygen is cut in half?

THE EARTH'S ATMOSPHERE IS MADE UP CHIEFLY OF FIVE GASSES: nitrogen, oxygen, water vapor, argon, and carbon dioxide. Air can contain as much as 5% water vapor, more commonly ranging from 1 to 3%.

The composition of air in percent by volume at sea level, at 15 degrees Centigrade, and 101325 Pascals of air pressure is:

- Nitrogen -- N2 -- 78.084%
- Oxygen -- O2 -- 20.9476%
- Argon -- Ar -- 0.934%
- Carbon Dioxide -- CO2 -- 0.0314%

If oxygen is reduced to 10 percent, air pressure changes. Nitrogen rises to 88%, filling the gap left by oxygen.

Day one

Human beings die. All mammals die, even whales, porpoises, and manatees. Birds die also. Insects are unaffected, except flying insects which must adjust to a change in air pressure.

Day five

Decomposition of mammalian and avian carcasses begins.

Day thirty

Decomposition is complete. Worms, slugs, and snails begin to work the material.

What if seeds do not germinate?

Day 1

SUGARCANE IS NOT AFFECTED. ALTHOUGH SOME SUGARCANES PRODUCE seeds, stem cutting is the most common reproduction method. Each cutting must contain at least one bud.

Cuttings are sometimes hand-planted. In more technologically advanced countries, billet planting is common. Stalks or stalk sections are planted by a machine that opens and recloses the ground.

Day 5

Marijuana growers learn that seeds will not germinate. They realize that their present plants are all they will have. They increase their prices tenfold for pot on hand, wait to set the price for pot yet to be harvested from extant plants.

Day 6

Opium growers also learn that poppy seeds will not germinate. They realize that their present plants are all they will have. They increase their prices twentyfold for opium on hand and fiftyfold for heroin and cocaine on hand. Their price for codeine is set at $500/gram.

Day 8

Methamphetamine and fentanyl production increase, along with their street prices.

Day 30

Farmers see that their wheat, rice, barley, corn, and soybeans have not sprouted.

Day 35

Because wine is propagated by cuttings, the future supply of wine, port, Cinzano, and all vermouths is stable. Stock market prices for publicly held wine companies increase. Privately held companies consider IPOs.

Liquor companies realize their present stocks of bourbon, scotch, and Irish whiskey are all they will ever have.

They raise prices for Jack Daniel's, Famous Grouse, and Bushmills. Prosperous homeowners stock up. Less prosperous people hoard beer.

Because both gin and vodka can be produced from fermented grapes, their supply is ultimately not in jeopardy. But because the process requires a lot of grapes, the prices of grapes rise worldwide. The prices of gin and vodka rise also.

Day 40

Stores have sold out of lettuce, carrots, peppers, eggplants, potatoes, tofu, and turnips. Homeowners build root cellars for their potatoes, which are propagated from pieces of potato each bearing an eye. The price of grain futures rises sharply. Stock markets anticipate problems for cereal makers and retailers of grain products.

Homeowners buy freezers, hoarding all beef, pork, and lamb they can buy. Stock prices of Lowe's and Home Depot rise.

In the third world, there is widespread starvation except where there are fish.

Day 45

Because the supply of fish is unaffected, consumption of fish rises.

Day 50

Consumers hoard boxed cereals, grits, all varieties of flour, and rice.

McDonald's, Arby's, and Sonic develop breadless products. Their stock market prices drop. French fry sales increase.

Day 55

Grafting of tomatoes, cucumbers, eggplants, and watermelon has begun. Japanese grafting robots for these herbaceous plants are in high demand.

Grafting of white spruce is accelerated. Grafting of other woody plants is attempted.

Day 60

Mainstream denomination church attendance rises. Chiliastic faiths see non-germination as the beginning of the millennium. Atheists see non-germination as proof there is no God.

Enrollment in seminaries and theological schools increases.

Day 90

Deaths from methamphetamine and fentanyl rise abruptly.,

Day 100

The Food Channel develops programs devoted to wild game.

Hunting increases. Shotgun and rifle sales increase. The stock prices of firearms companies rise.

Clover and ryegrass have died out.

Because zoysia propagates without seed, vegetarians begin to eat zoysia.

Efforts begin with fermentation of zoysia. There is still wild yeast in the air. The fermentation is successful.

Day 120

Lumber prices rise sharply. Volunteers scour the world for young oak, hickory, walnut, maple, and cherry trees to transplant.

Maple trees continue to produce sap for maple syrup for another fifty years. But unlike wine, there are no rootstocks for grafting.

"Building with bamboo" shows appear on do-it-yourself channels.

Day 180

"Zoybooze" is a wildly successful IPO.

Day 220

Marijuana growers announce price for weed from their extant (and final) plants, at $1000/gram.

Day 240

Budweiser purchases a majority holding in Zoybooze.

Day 245

Coors files a restraint of trade lawsuit against Budweiser in Colorado federal court, asking for a temporary injunction *pendente lite*.

Day 250

The Colorado federal court denies the temporary injunction, but indicates it will hold a prompt hearing.

Day 300

The Colorado federal court finds Budweiser's exclusive control of Zoybooze is "not reasonably necessary."

Coors promptly buys 1000 gallons of Zoybooze.

Budweiser and Coors, having no beer to sell, begin marketing of soda drinks containing Zoybooze.

What if the world's primary documents came only from my memory?

You might find it interesting how much your own list varies from mine.

By primary documents, I mean the real things, the texts themselves, not our memory of what is in them. Memorization was done in Ray Bradbury's *Fahrenheit 451* (1953) by individual men because of book burnings by salamanders. Each man was responsible for memorizing one or more author's complete works.

If I were in that role, the world would have an odd list, and a short one. The world would be much poorer, and perhaps amused. It would have:

Part of *Rocky Top*:

> Corn won't grow at all on Rock Top.
> Dirt's too rocky by far.
> That's why all the folks on Rocky Top
> Get their corn from a jar.
> Rocky Top, you'll always be
> Home sweet home to me.
> Good ole' Rocky Top,
> Rocky Top, Tennessee.
> Rocky Top, Tennessee.

The start of James Russell Lowell's hymn, *Once to Every Man and Nation* (1845)

> Once to every man and nation
> Comes the moment to decide,
> In the strife of truth with falsehood,
> For the good or evil side . . .

Clement Moore's *'Twas the Night Before Christmas* (1822):

Twas the night before Christmas, when all through the
house
Not a creature was stirring, not even a mouse;
The stockings were hung by the chimney with care,
In hopes that St. Nicholas soon would be there;
The children were nestled all snug in their beds,
While visions of sugar-plums danced in their heads;
And mamma in her kerchief, and I in my cap,
Had just settled down for a long winter's nap,
When out on the lawn there arose such a clatter,
I sprang from the bed to see what was the matter.
Away to the window, I flew like a flash,
Tore open the shutters and threw up the sash.
The moon on the breast of the new-fallen snow
Gave the luster of midday to objects below,
When what to my wondering eyes should appear,
But a miniature sleigh, and eight tiny reindeer,
With a little old driver, so lively and quick,
I knew in a moment it must be St. Nick.
More rapid than eagles his coursers they came,
And he whistled, and shouted, and called them by name;
"Now, Dasher! Now, Dancer! Now, Prancer And Vixen!
On, Comet! On Cupid! On, Donner And Blitzen!
To the top of the porch! to the top of the wall!
Now dash away! dash away! dash away all!"
As dry leaves that before the wild hurricane fly,
When they meet with an obstacle, mount to the sky,
So up to the house-top the coursers they flew,
With the sleigh full of toys, and St. Nicholas too.
And then, in a twinkling, I heard on the roof
The prancing and pawing of each little hoof.
As I drew in my hand and was turning around,
Down the chimney St. Nicholas came with a bound.
He was dressed all in fur, from his head to his foot,

And his clothes were all tarnished with ashes and soot;
A bundle of toys he had flung on his back,
And he looked like a peddler just opening his pack.
His eyes--how they twinkled! his dimples how merry!
His cheeks were like roses, his nose like a cherry!
His droll little mouth was drawn up like a bow,
And the beard of his chin was as white as the snow;
The stump of a pipe he held tight in his teeth,
And the smoke it encircled his head like a wreath;
He had a broad face and a little round belly,
That shook when he laughed like a bowlful of jelly.
He was chubby and plump, a right jolly old elf,
And I laughed when I saw him, in spite of myself;
A wink of his eye and a twist of his head,
Soon gave me to know I had nothing to dread;
He spoke not a word, but went straight to his work,
And filled all the stockings; then turned with a jerk,
And laying his finger aside of his nose,
And giving a nod, up the chimney he rose;
He sprang to his sleigh, to his team gave a whistle,
And away they all flew like the down of a thistle.
But I heard him exclaim, ere he drove out of sight,
Happy Christmas To All, And To All A Good-night!

The Lord's Prayer from Matthew chapter six:

Our Father, who art in heaven, hallowed be thy name;
thy kingdom come; thy will be done; on earth as it is
in heaven.
Give us this day our daily bread.
And forgive us our trespasses,
as we forgive those who trespass against us.
And lead us not into temptation;
but deliver us from evil.
For thine is the kingdom, the power and the glory, for ever.
Amen.

The 1611 King James text of the birth narrative in *Luke 2*:

And it came to pass in those days, that there went out a decree from Caesar Augustus that all the world should be taxed. (And this taxing was first made when Cyrenius was governor of Syria.) And all went to be taxed, every one into his own city.

And Joseph also went up from Galilee, out of the city of Nazareth, into Judaea, unto the city of David, which is called Bethlehem (because he was of the house and lineage of David) to be taxed with Mary, his espoused wife, being great with child.

And so it was, that, while they were there, the days were accomplished that she should be delivered.

And she brought forth her firstborn son, and wrapped him in swaddling clothes, and laid him in a manger; because there was no room for them in the inn.

And there were in the same country shepherds abiding in the field, keeping watch over their flock by night.

And, lo, the angel of the Lord came upon them, and the glory of the Lord shone round about them: and they were sore afraid.

And the angel said unto them, "Fear not: for, behold, I bring you good tidings of great joy, which shall be to all people.

For unto you is born this day in the city of David a Savior, which is Christ the Lord.

And this shall be a sign unto you;

Ye shall find the babe wrapped in swaddling clothes, lying in a manger."

And suddenly there was with the angel a multitude of the heavenly host praising God, and saying,

"Glory to God in the highest, and on earth peace, good will toward men."

Goethe's *Koenig in Thule* (1774):

Es war ein König in Thule,
Gar treu bis an das Grab,
Dem sterbend seine Buhle
Einen goldnen Becher gab.
Es ging ihm nichts darüber,
Er leert' ihn jeden Schmaus;
Die Augen gingen ihm über,
So oft er trank daraus.
Und als er kam zu sterben,
Zählt' er seine Städt' im Reich,
Gönnt' alles seinen Erben,
Den Becher nicht zugleich.
Er saß bei'm Königsmahle,
Die Ritter um ihn her,
Auf hohem Vätersaale,
Dort auf dem Schloß am Meer.
Dort stand der alte Zecher,
Trank letzte Lebensgluth,
Und warf den heiligen Becher
Hinunter in die Fluth.
Er sah ihn stürzen, trinken
Und sinken tief ins Meer,
Die Augen thäten ihm sinken,
Trank nie einen Tropfen mehr.

There was a king in Thule,
Was faithful till the grave,
To whom his mistress, dying,
A golden goblet gave.

Nought was to him more precious;
He drained it at every bout;
His eyes with tears ran over,
As oft as he drank thereout.

When came his time of dying,
The towns in his land he told,
Nought else to his heir denying
Except the goblet of gold.

He sat at the royal banquet
With his knights of high degree,
In the lofty hall of his fathers
In the castle by the sea.

There stood the old carouser,
And drank the last life-glow;
And hurled the hallowed goblet
Into the tide below.

He saw it plunging and filling,
And sinking deep in the sea:
Then fell his eyelids for ever,
And never more drank he!

The King James text of the *23d Psalm*:

The LORD *is* my shepherd; I shall not want.

He maketh me to lie down in green pastures: he leadeth
me beside the still waters.

He restoreth my soul: he leadeth me in the paths of righteousness for his name's sake.

Yea, though I walk through the valley of the shadow of death, I will fear no evil: for thou *art* with me; thy rod and thy staff they comfort me.

Thou preparest a table before me in the presence of mine enemies: thou anointest my head with oil; my cup runneth over.

Surely goodness and mercy shall follow me all the days of my life: and I will dwell in the house of the LORD for ever.

The King James text of the *100ᵗʰ Psalm:*

Make a joyful noise unto the Lord, all ye lands.

Serve the Lord with gladness: come before his presence with singing.

Know ye that the Lord he is God: it is he that hath made us, and not we ourselves; we are his people, and the sheep of his pasture.

Enter into his gates with thanksgiving, and into his courts with praise: be thankful unto him, and bless his name.

For the Lord is good; his mercy is everlasting; and his truth endureth to all generations.

The most important verse in the Bible:

For God so loved the world, that he gave his only begotten Son, that whosoever believeth in him should not perish, but have everlasting life.

Thomas Ken's *doxology* (1709):

Praise God, from whom all blessings flow;
Praise Him, all creatures here below;
Praise Him above, ye heavenly host;
Praise Father, Son, and Holy Ghost.

The start of Kafka's *Der Prozeß* (1914):

Jemand musste Josef K. verleumdet haben, denn ohne dass er etwas Böses getan hätte, wurde er eines Morgens verhaftet.

Someone must have been telling tales about Josef K., for one morning, without having done anything wrong, he was arrested.

Two passages from the Episcopal *Book of Common Prayer* (1662):

The peace of God which passeth all understanding, keep your hearts and minds in the knowledge and love of God, and of his son Jesus Christ our Lord.

And the blessing of God Almighty, the Father, the Son, and the holy Ghost, be amongst you, and remain with you always.

We acknowledge and bewail our manifold sins and wickedness, which We from time to time most grievously have committed, By thought word, and deed, Against thy divine Majesty, Provoking most justly thy wrath and indignation against us.

We do earnestly repent, and are heartily sorry for these our misdoings . . .

Jane Austen, *Pride and Prejudice*:

It is a truth universally acknowledged, that a single man in possession of a good fortune, must be in want of a wife.

A nursery rhyme riddle:

As I was going to St. Ives,
I met a man with seven wives,
Each wife had seven sacks,
Each sack had seven cats,
Each cat had seven kits:
Kits, cats, sacks, and wives,
How many were there going to St Ives?

The start of this Christmas carol:

O Tannenbaum, o Tannenbaum,
wie treu sind deine Blätter!
Du grünst nicht nur zur Sommerzeit,
Nein auch im Winter, wenn es schneit.
O Tannenbaum, o Tannenbaum,
wie treu sind deine Blätter!

O Christmas tree, o Christmas tree
How loyal are your leaves!
You're green not only in the summertime,
No, also in winter when it snows.
O Christmas tree, o Christmas tree
How loyal are your leaves!

A limerick:

> There was an old man from Nantucket
> Who kept all his cash in a bucket.
> His daughter named Nan
> Ran away with a man,
> And as for the cash, Nan tuck it.

An Everly brothers song:

> Wake up, little Susie, wake up.
> Wake up, little Susie, wake up.
> We've both been sound asleep
> Wake up little Susie and weep.
> The movie's over, it's four o'clock
> And we're in trouble deep.
> Wake up, little Susie,
> Wake up, little Susie.
> Well, what are we gonna tell your Mama?
> What are we gonna tell your Pa?
> What are we gonna tell our friends
> When they say, "Ooh la la!"
> Wake up, little Susie,
> Wake up, little Susie.
> Well, I told your Mama that you'd be in by ten
> Well, Susie baby, looks like we goofed again.
> Wake up, little Susie,
> Wake up, little Susie.
> We gotta go home.
> Wake up, little Susie, wake up.
> Wake up, little Susie, wake up.
> The movie wasn't so hot.
> It didn't have much of a plot
> We fell asleep, our goose is cooked
> Our reputation is shot.

The beginning of John Mason Neale's *Good King Wenceslas* (1853):

> Good King Wenceslas looked out,
> On the Feast of Stephen,
> When the snow lay round about,
> Deep and crisp and even;
> Brightly shone the moon that night,
> though the frost was cruel
> When a poor man came in sight,
> Gathering winter fuel.

Robert Frost (1874-1963), *Stopping by Woods on a Snowy Evening*:

> Whose woods these are I think I know.
> His house is in the village, though;
> He will not see me stopping here
> To watch his woods fill up with snow.
> My little horse must think it queer
> To stop without a farmhouse near
> Between the woods and frozen lake
> The darkest evening of the year.
> He gives his harness bells a shake
> To ask if there is some mistake.
> The only other sound's the sweep
> Of easy wind and downy flake.
> The woods are lovely, dark and deep,
> But I have promises to keep,
> And miles to go before I sleep,
> And miles to go before I sleep.

This poem glides along easily despite having a highly structured rhyming scheme: aaba bbcb ccdc dddd. Perhaps our speaker has Christmas presents to deliver? It is the 21st of December ("the darkest evening of the year").

Robert Frost, *Dust of Snow*

> The way a crow shook down on me
> Dust of snow from a hemlock tree
> Has given my heart a change of mood
> And saved some part
> Of a day I had rued.

Robert Bryan (1931-2018) and Marshall Dodge (1935-1982), *The Body in the Kelp:*

> We were clammin' along the beach one Sunday when
> we come upon a body in the kelp. We didn't recognize
> the face, but thought it might have been old John, who
> tended the lighthouse on the point. We went directly out
> and knocked on John's door.
> "You there, John?"
> "Damn right I'm here. What can I do for you?"
> "We found a body down in the kelp. Thought it might
> have been you." "Wearin' a red shirt?"
> "Yessir, red shirt."
> "Blue trousers?"
> "They were blue trousers."
> "Rubber boots?"
> "Ayup, rubber boots."
> "Was they high or low?"
> "They was low boots."
> "You sure?"
> "Well, come to think of it, they were high boots turned
> down low."
> "Oh, well then, twern't me."

Goethe's *Wanderers Nachtlied:*

> Über allen Gipfeln Ist Ruh,
> In allen Wipfeln spürest du
> Kaum einen Hauch;

Die Vögelein schweigen im Walde.
Warte nur, balde
Ruhest du auch.

O'er all the hilltops
Is quiet now,
In all the treetops
Hearest thou
Hardly a breath;
The birds are asleep in the trees:
Wait, soon like these
Thou too shalt rest.
(*Translation by Henry Wadsworth Longfellow*)

The beginning of Poe's *Raven*:

Once upon a midnight dreary, while I pondered, weak
and weary,
Over many a quaint and curious volume of forgotten lore—
While I nodded, nearly napping, suddenly there came
a tapping,
As of some one gently rapping, rapping at my chamber
door.
"'Tis some visitor," I muttered, "tapping at my chamber
door—
Only this and nothing more."

Shakespeare's *Romeo and Juliet*:

ABRAHAM: Do you bite your thumb at us, sir?
SAMPSON: I do bite my thumb, sir.
ABRAHAM: Do you bite your thumb at us, sir?
SAMPSON: No, sir, I do not bite my thumb at you, sir,
but I bite my thumb, sir.

Some nursery rhymes:

Little Bo Peep:
Little Bo-Peep has lost her sheep,
And doesn't know where to find them;
Leave them alone, and they'll come home,
dragging their tails behind them.

Little Boy Blue:
Little Boy Blue,
Come blow your horn.
The sheep's in the meadow,
The cow's in the corn.
Where is the little boy
Who looks after the sheep?
He's under the haystack
Fast asleep.

Little Jack Horner:
Little Jack Horner
Sat in the corner,
Eating a Christmas pie;
He put in his thumb,
And pulled out a plum,
And said, "What a good boy am I."

Jack Sprat:
Jack Sprat could eat no fat.
His wife could eat no lean.
And so between them both you see
They licked the platter clean.

Wee Willy Winky:
Wee Willie Winkie runs through the town,
Upstairs and downstairs in his night-gown,
Tapping at the window, crying at the lock,
Are the children in their bed, for it's past ten o'clock?

Old Mother Hubbard:
Old Mother Hubbard
Went to the cupboard
To get her poor dog a bone;
But when she got there,
The cupboard was bare,
And so the poor dog had none.

Jack and Jill:
Jack and Jill went up the hill
To fetch a pail of water.
Jack fell down and broke his crown,
And Jill came tumbling after.

The Old Woman Who Lived in a Shoe:
There was an old woman who lived in a shoe.
She had so many children, she didn't know what to do.
She gave them some broth without any bread;
And whipped them all soundly and put them to bed.

The Queen of Hearts, She Made Some Tarts:
The Queen of Hearts, she made some tarts,
All on a summer's day;
The knave of Hearts, he stole the tarts,
And took them clean away.

Ride a Cock Horse to Banbury Cross:
Ride a cock-horse to Banbury Cross,
To see a fine lady upon a white horse;
Rings on her fingers and bells on her toes,
And she shall have music wherever she goes.

Little Miss Muffet:
Little Miss Muffet
Sat on a tuffet,
Eating her curds and whey;

Along came a spider,
Who sat down beside her,
And frightened Miss Muffet away.

Two passages from Goethe's *Faust I* (1805):

> Habe nun, ach! Philosophie,
> Juristerei und Medizin,
> Und leider auch Theologie
> Durchaus studiert, mit heißem Bemühn.
> Da steh ich nun, ich armer Tor!
> Und bin so klug als wie zuvor;
> Heiße Magister, heiße Doktor gar
> Und ziehe schon an die zehen Jahr
> Herauf, herab und quer und krumm
> Meine Schüler an der Nase herum--
> Und sehe, daß wir nichts wissen können!

> Well, that's Philosophy I've read,
> And Law and Medicine,
> and I fear Theology too, from A to Z;
> Hard studies all, that have cost me dear.
> And so I sit, poor silly man,
> No wiser now than when I began.
> They call me Professor and Doctor, forsooth,
> For misleading many an innocent youth
> These last ten years now,
> Pulling them to and fro by the nose;
> And I see all our search for knowledge is vain.

> Werd ich zum Augenblicke sagen:
> Verweile doch! du bist so schön!
> Dann magst du mich in Fesseln schlagen,
> Dann will ich gern zugrunde gehn!

If ever to the moment I shall say:
Beautiful moment, do not pass away!
Then you may forge your chains to bind me,
Then I will put my life behind me.

The beginning of Longfellow's *Evangeline:*

This is the forest primeval.
The murmuring pines and the hemlocks,
Bearded with moss, and in garments green, indistinct
in the twilight,
Stand like Druids of eld, with voices sad and prophetic,
Stand like harpers hoar, with beards that rest on their
bosoms.

A toe-naming game for children:

This little piggy went to market.
This little piggy stayed home.
This little piggy had roast beef.
This little piggy had none.
And this little piggy cried,
"Wee, wee, wee," all the way home.

The beginning of Tennyson's *Tithonus* (1859):

The woods decay, the woods decay and fall,
The vapors weep their burthen to the ground,
Man comes and tills the field and lies beneath,
And after many a summer dies the swan.

Part of A.A. Milne's 1926 *Winnie the Pooh:*

> "It all comes," said Pooh crossly, "of not having front doors big enough."

> "It all comes," said Rabbit sternly, "of eating too much. I thought at the time," said Rabbit, "only I didn't like to say anything," said Rabbit, "that one of us was eating too much, and I knew it wasn't *me.*"

A passage from Lewis Carrol's *Through the Looking Glass:*

> *'Twas brillig, and the slithy toves*
> *Did gyre and gimble in the wabe:*
> *All mimsy were the borogoves,*
> *And the mome raths outgrabe.*

The beginning of Heine's *Lorelei* (1823):

> Ich weiß nicht, was soll es bedeuten,
> Daß ich so traurig bin;
> Ein Märchen aus alten Zeiten,
> Das kommt mir nicht aus dem Sinn.

> I don't know what it means
> That I am so sad
> A legend of bygone days
> That I cannot keep out of my mind.

Two Harvard songs:

> Fair Harvard! Thy sons to thy Jubilee throng,
> And with blessings surrender thee o'er,
> By these festival rites, from the age that is past,
> To the age that is waiting before.
> O relic and type of our ancestors' worth
> That hast long kept their memory warm,

First flow'r of their wilderness!
Star of their night!
Calm rising thro' change and thro' storm.

With crimson in triumph flashing,
Mid the strains of victory,
Poor Eli's hopes we are dashing
Into blue obscurity.
Resistless our team sweeps goal-ward,
With the fury of the blast,
We'll fight for the name of Harvard
Till the last white line is passed.

The start of Yeats's *Innisfree* (1888):

I will arise and go now, and go to Innisfree,
And a small cabin build there, of clay and wattles made;
Nine bean-rows will I have there, a hive for the honey-bee,
And live alone in the bee-loud glade.

A Christmas melody:

Christmas is a'comin'
And the goose is getting fat.
Please to put a penny
In the old man's hat.
If you haven't got a penny,
Then a ha'penny will do.
If you haven't got a ha'penny,
Then God bless you.
God bless you, Gentleman,
God bless you.
If you haven't got a ha'penny,
Then God bless you.

What if 22 hours in a day?

Day 1

CHILDREN DO NOT NOTICE THE CHANGE.

No adult understands how it could have happened, but two hours are missing from every day. Gloom and discouragement abound. Some adults give up, quit their jobs. Others buckle down, trying to accomplish more in the time available. On balance there is a net loss in productivity.

Day 10

Television and radio stations adjust staffing to new schedules. They terminate many workers.

Day 20

In developed countries with independent legal systems, class action suits are filed against the employers.

Day 25

London's Big Ben and all other analog clocks simply are set to noon, and the works stopped.

Day 28

The discouragement leads to an increase in suicides. The Malthusian Society issues a statement of praise, and reminds everyone of Thomas Robert Malthus's birthday, February 13.

Day 30

The world's gross domestic product has fallen off by 5 percent. Stock prices slip.

Day 35

In those developed countries which have independent legal systems, employers respond with "act of God" defense.

Day 40

Makers of analog clocks decline to produce 22-hour clocks, deciding to leave the new timekeeping to smart phones.

Owners of wrist watches take them off. Lawyers turn from Rolexes to Porsches, Jaguars, and Maseratis to demonstrate social status.

Day 80

The Rolex Company and 49 other Swiss watch companies go out of business. The GDP of Switzerland decreases 30%.

What if 26 hours in a day?

Day 1

JOY IN THE HEARTS OF ALL WORKAHOLICS. TASKS ARE TACKLED AND conquered. New tasks are undertaken. The workaholics' lament has been answered that there just aren't enough hours in the day.

Day 25

London's Big Ben and all other analog clocks simply are set to noon, and the works stopped.

Day 30

The gross domestic product increases in the U.S. so significantly that stock prices rise across the board. GDP also rises in other developed countries.

GDP does not rise in primitive countries. They find the new length of day simply odd.

Day 40

Makers of analog clocks decline to produce 26-hour clocks, deciding to leave the new timekeeping to smart phones.

Owners of wrist watches take them off.

Lawyers turn from Rolexes to Porsches, Jaguars, and Maseratis to demonstrate social status.

Day 80

The Rolex Company and 49 other Swiss watch companies go out of business. The GDP of Switzerland decreases 30%.

What if there is half gravity?

Mass and weight are different. At half gravity things weigh less, but their mass is the same. On a half-gravity planet, what would weigh 60 pounds on earth, will weigh 30 pounds.

If two cars run head-on into each other at 70 mph, the damage is the same at half gravity and full gravity, because the damage depends upon mass, not weight. Interestingly, it is much harder to get the cars up to that 70 mph, because the lesser gravity affects traction.

If you jump on the moon with its 1/6 gravity, you will jump six times higher than on earth. On mars, with its 1/3 gravity, you will jump three times higher than on earth. On a half-gravity planet, you will jump twice as high as on earth.

Over generations, people will grow taller.

Plants will immediately grow taller, but they will grow just fine. Trees might blow over in a wind, depending on how well their root structure can hold itself in the soil.

On earth, a column of air exists 62 miles high; this produces 15 pounds per square inch of air pressure. But at half gravity, that column of air weighs half as much.

Airplane "lift" is affected. On earth, it is easier to take off in Charleston, SC (sea level) than in Denver, CO (5000 feet high). On a half-gravity planet, you need larger wing surfaces or greater speed, or both. It all depends on air pressure, not on gravity. This then gets complicated: lower air pressure makes it harder to take off, but lower gravity makes it easier to take off. To figure out the sweet spot will take a lot of mathematics.

Helicopters will need larger blades. Historical fact: in Afghanistan, helicopters could not fly to get to Bin Laden. The air was too thin.

Trains and cars will not use less fuel, because pushing something on the ground depends on mass (which is unchanged) not weight.

The same applies to river and ocean traffic.

But the waves in the ocean will get much bigger. On our planet, waves extend 30 feet up and 30 feet down. But at half gravity, that will be doubled. Beach flora and fauna will be physically disrupted.

Nuclear reactors are not affected, because the coolant is pumped.

Baseball will be affected. Sinkers will not sink, and curves might not curve as much. Fastballs are unchanged.

Mammalian fertility is unaffected. Sperm swims fine in the water.

With scuba diving you will be able to go deeper and stay longer, because the water around you weighs less.

Tigers will be able to jump out of their zoo enclosures. They weigh half as much. But if they run into a wall (mass being unchanged), their body damage is the same as at full gravity.

Your garage door is lifted by a spring calibrated to lift the weight of the door. The door weighs half as much on a half gravity planet. So, if you trigger your garage door opener, the door will fly up, smash against whatever is at the end of the rails, and be damaged.

"Pogo sticks" will jump twice as high.

What if the sun is at half strength?

Day 1

THE SUN IS SUDDENLY AT HALF STRENGTH. IT RISES AND SETS AS USUAL, but it is only half as bright and only half as warm.

Day 30

The polar ice caps have doubled. The Gulf Stream has changed course. There is no longer an *el Niño* or *la Niña*.

Day 60

Glaciers have crept southward over North America and Asia. And north over South America. Animals and humans move to avoid the cold. Stock markets gyrate wildly.

Day 365

The entire planet is frozen. Mammalian land life ends.

Day 4000

The oceans have frozen down to the seabed. All life ends, except for unicellular organisms in the seabed soil.

English is a tough language: Part One

IF YOU ARE FORTUNATE ENOUGH TO BE BORN INTO ENGLISH, YOU HAVE an enormous blessing. Not just because it is the world's language of commerce, which of course it is. It's because English is a difficult language.

It is a beast to learn for those people who are not born into the language. Logic "just ain't in it." To begin with, there are "strong" verbs, the ones that change their stem vowels. *Throw, threw, thrown. See, saw, seen,* and so forth. As English-speaking children make their way to adulthood, their parents repeatedly correct them with these difficult past tenses.

The children understand past tenses and want to use them. So on their own they try to use "weak" verbs, the ones that do not change their stem vowels. They simply make them up: *I throwed the ball, I seed him at school.* At this point, parents and school teachers step in to teach children proper language.

If you can see Spanish, you can say it. And--how about this?--you can also spell it. Same for German. If you can see the German word, you can say it, and you can spell it. Not so much for French, at least for pronunciation. And no way for English. Think about our magnificent words "though" and "tough." Or our "cough. And our "through." And "take," "ache," and "steak." All spelled differently but with the vowel sounds identical.

So when our children begin to read, the obstacles are huge. Enter stage right, with trumpets, parents, and school teachers.

English is a tough language: Part Two

AFTER PARENTS AND SCHOOL TEACHERS HAVE DONE THEIR GOOD WORK, the children are well along in reading.

This is so despite the minefields of *though, tough, cough,* and *through.* The children have learned that they simply have to treat those nasties as "sight words" to be memorized. No logic, no sounding them out.

And then things got worse. More nasties appeared: *aught, bought, fraught, thought, slaughter, laughter, slough.* What to do? There is simply no hope. They also have to be "sight words." No way around it. Memorize them.

This is not good, but it is the way of the world in English. Do you begin to feel good about being born into English? You should. Think of the folks for whom English is a Second Language (ESL).

This rhyme can drive you and them crazy:

> *The snake thought aught*
> *but that he ought*
> *go slough his doughy skin.*

It sounds like something from Lewis Carrol's *"Jabberwocky"*

> *'Twas brillig, and the slithy toves*
> *Did gyre and gimble in the wabe:*
> *All mimsy were the borogoves,*
> *And the mome raths outgrabe.*

Happily, this Jabberwocky passage has no real world meaning. It is compartmentalized nonsense.

But for our children and for the ESL folks, the snake rhyme does have meaning.

English homophones

DO NOT GET LOST IN THE TERMINOLOGY OF HOMOPHONES AND THEIR linguistic kin--the homographs, homonyms, synonyms, heteronyms, etc. It is a huge morass of terms which can leave you feeling inadequate. There are even Venn diagrams which seek to explain the morass. All of this is unnecessary.

The only things to remember are:

a. "homo" means the same
b. "phone" means sound
c. "graph" means writing
d. "nym" means name

If you are armed with those concepts, you can navigate all the foolishness that is written about this overdeveloped linguistic landscape.

Here are a few homophones (things that sound alike):

> Rain reign rein
> Brake break
> Creek creak
> Rose rose rows
> Paste paced
> Sear sere
> Deer dear
> Bawl ball
> Rabbit rabbet
> Bust bussed
> Trust trussed
> Mussed must
> Tail tale
> Sail sale
> Pain pane

Bore boar
Reek wreak
Wrought rot
Whore hoar
Their there they're

The list could go on and on. There is even a website which lists the twenty-five homophones most important for non-native English speakers.

George Orwell's 1946 Writing Rules

BEFORE ORWELL'S 1946 RULES, THERE WAS WILLIAM STRUNK JR. (1869-1946).

Strunk first used his own book, *The Elements of Style*, in 1919, privately publishing it for use at Cornell University. Harcourt published it in 1920. Strunk's son Oliver published it again in 1935.

In 1919 E. B. White was a student in Professor Strunk's class at Cornell, where he used "the little book" for himself. Macmillan commissioned him to revise it. White edited the 1959 and 1972 editions of *The Elements of Style*.

In "Politics and the English language," (1946) Orwell teaches:

1. Never use a metaphor, simile or other figure of speech which you are used to seeing in print.
2. Never use a long word where a short one will do.
3. If it is possible to cut a word out, always cut it out.
4. Never use the passive where you can use the active.
5. Never use a foreign phrase, a scientific word or a jargon word if you can think of an everyday English equivalent.
6. Break any of these rules sooner than say anything outright barbarous.

Language 1:
If you can see it, you can say it

ONE OF THE GOOD THINGS ABOUT GERMAN AND SPANISH IS THAT IF you have the written word, you can pronounce it. The pronunciation s absolutely reliable.

Not so in French. If you can see it, you can only maybe say it. Additionally, the French language is famously ambiguous. It is said that is why French is the language of diplomacy.

Now in English, it is sadly <u>not</u> true that you can say it just by looking at the written word. It is often true. It is true often enough to mislead you, but there are daunting exceptions. Consider:

> "Cough," where the vowel sound rhymes with "off"
> "Enough," where the vowel sound rhymes with "fluff"
> "Bough," (of a tree), and "Slough," (muddy wet place, or figuratively, a slough of despond), where the vowel sound rhymes with "cow"
> "Through," where the vowel sound rhymes with "goo"
> "Thought," where the vowel sound rhymes with "hot"
> "Though," where the vowel sound rhymes with "go"

Speaking local revisited

In my 2021 book "Kirksey" I looked at some local sayings. As time has passed since writing that book, even more localisms have turned up. Here are some of them:

"He was real keerful on the chance they was a snake the other side of the log."

"Keerful" = careful.

"They was" = there was.

"Saved my bacon" = rescued me.

"Kindly" = "somewhat" = "kind of"

"I'ze 'ginnin' to think . . ." = "I was beginning to think . . ." Usually used with a phrase meaning the speaker almost erroneously believed a certain thing.

"It's daggon/dadgum dry." = "It is really very dry."

"Out the wazoo" = a lot of something.

"Puppies" means (aside from immature dogs) simply "things." Combining these two entries, one can hear, "I got them puppies out the wazoo." Which means, "I really have a lot of those things."

"Sell/sale." This is a matter of pronunciation. For many East Tennesseeans the words are pronounced the same. This is unfortunate, and ignorant, but there it is. An item is "for sell" if you want to dispose of it at a price. There is always a giant "Labor Day Sell" advertised by radio and TV. In print, the newspaper does get it right: "Labor Day Sale." I have not heard it yet, but I imagine some day I will hear, "The sellboat has two masts."

"I ain't seed bear one for five months." = "I haven't seen any bears at all for five months." "Bear one" is an interesting formulation. It could also be used for any other visible thing, for example, "Chevy one." "I ain't seed Chevy one." ("I haven't seen any cars of the Chevrolet brand.")

"Nary," meaning "none." ("I got nary butter. I need to go to the store and get me some.") Nary is an adjective in that sentence. But it can stand alone as a noun: "Have you got any honey left? I got nary."

"Listen atcha" means, "Just listen to you." (An expression of wonderment)

"Hink": "I walk well with two trekking poles, but with only one I just hink along." (Hink is an old word, probably of Scandinavian origin; akin to Old Norse *hinkr*, hesitation, from *hinka* to limp; Middle Low German *hinken*; Old English *hincian*, to limp; Old High German *hinkan*, to limp; Old Norse *skakkr*, crooked, askew.)

"I'm over it." = "I've had enough of this." "I'm done with it." "I am disgusted."

"Not perzackly" = not exactly

"Don't knows I can do it," (and "don't knows as how I can do it") mean, "I am not sure I can do it."

"That's a mite precarious." = A bit risky.

"I've gotta splinker in my thumb." Splinker = splinter. "I have a splinter in my thumb."

"I'm gonna kill me some yellow jackets." What is interesting in this statement is "me," in the dative case. It is an indirect object of the transitive verb "kill." The dative in this construction is often called the dative of advantage or disadvantage, denoting the person or thing for whose benefit or to whose prejudice the action is performed. It occurs in both Latin and German.

"He'll turn you ever' which way but loose." = "You are never going to get shet of him." "Shet" = shed = "rid of"

"Mad as a wet hen," is commonly said, and you would think that it must describe reality. It doesn't. My hens wander around in the rain even when they could be dry inside their house.

"Purt near" = pretty near; almost

"That wadn't bad." = "That was pretty good." Here the negative is used to yield a positive.

"Gwine to do": "I'm gwine to do that, first chanct I git."

"Crooked as a snake" = "extremely dishonest"

"Roon" = ruin. Roon is used as a verb, never as a noun. "If'n you put your sharp knives in the dishwasher, it'll roon 'em."

"Blarey" = "blurry" This word may be a combination of "glare" and "blur."

"That's just mizzibl." = "That is simply miserable, really too bad, regrettable."

"I'm gone kick yo' ass." The word "gone" here rhymes with tone, bone, and cone. "Gone" = gonna = going to.

"As slick as owl grease" = extremely excellent. The expression is popular throughout the South, but possibly originated in Texas. "Alcalde oil is as slick as owl grease" was cited in Texas newspapers in 1894. A 1931 list of questions about popular expressions asked, "How slick is owl grease?"

"Fast as greased lightning" means simply extremely fast.

"Crazy as a jaybird" = extremely crazy

"Right smuck in the middle" "Smuck" here is used alternatively to "smack." Both the words mean "exactly in the middle."

"Getting nowhere fast" = making no progress, spinning your wheels in the sand.

"They seen you comin'" means, "They knew they could take advantage of you, so they fleeced you." To "fleece someone" is to take his money. An example is the "fish" in a poker game, the guy who is invited because he is known to lose.

"Not worth a tinker's damn" There is disagreement regarding the spelling. Some claim it is *tinker's dam* while others say it should be *tinker's damn*. A tinker travels from one place to another repairing small things like utensils. An early definition of *tinker's dam*, recorded in the year 1877, stated that a tinker's dam was a piece of doughy material that tinkers used to hold metal in place when repairing it. The idea was that this material was worthless once the repair was complete, since it couldn't be reused and could serve no alternative purpose. However, other early versions of this idiom include *a tinker's curse* and *a tinker's cuss*. Apparently, back when being a tinker was a common profession, there was a stereotype that tinkers cursed often. If so, then the severity or importance of each curse would be small.

"All swole up": "He was all swole up from them bee stangs." *Swole* has existed in English since at least the early 1900s. It is used as another word for *swelled* or *swollen*. This is generally used when a part of someone's body has swelled from some type of affliction. This could be from allergies, toxins, being beaten up, or other causes.

Sep'n I could" = "This is going to be hard to do, sep'n I could do it t'other way round." ("If I do the other way, it will be easy.")

"Tard" = tired

"Truck with" = have to do with. "I'll have no truck with that nonsense."

"Out of kilter" = askew. "There's something out of kilter here."

"Hellacious" = extremely, awfully. "This is hellacious good chili."

"Tarnation" = damnation, hell. Usually with "in." "What in tarnation were you thinking?"

"Gumpshun" = gumption = courage

"Cattywampus" = crooked, out of kilter

"Piss poor" = extremely poor

"A pot to piss in": "He was so poor he didn't have a pot to piss in." This phrase may go back to the times of chamber pots.

"You're pissin' out." This means, "You are giving up, have lost your motivation, you are tired." It does not mean to urinate in the outward direction.

"Piss off!" is an exclamation meaning, "Get lost, go away, don't bother me."

"Pissed off": To be "pissed off" is a condition of vexation.

"Skeezix": an imaginary body part. "Be careful or you'll break your skeezix."

"Summer's": "It's here summer's." = "It is here somewhere."

"A piece of work": a fool, a person out of step. "He is a piece of work."

"A mort of trouble" = a lot of trouble. "Mort" means a great number, and was first used as such in 1694.

"Sucking wind" = accomplishing nothing, being out of luck. This saying probably derives from the anatomical pneumothorax.

"Fit to be tied": frustrated, upset, out of options

"Fine as frog's hair" means extremely excellent. It has nothing to do with the thinness of the filaments.

"Let's nail it." = "Let's do it, let's get it done."

"Auint and Airnt" are guttural sounds. They mean, "All right, OK, what's next, so?"

"Puckerbrush = scrubby bushes, thin bushes

"Front/back stoop" = a small porch. It comes from Middle Dutch.

"I flang it." = "I flung it." The Oxford English Dictionary notes "flang" as a dialectical past tense for fling.

"All tuckered out" = very tired: "I was real tard."

"I ran 'til my tongue was hangin out." = "I ran until I was exhausted." This may come from observing dogs.

"Damnfool" is pronounced the same way as "Coldbeer": The emphasis must be on the first syllable.

"Positively whipped" means completely whipped, completely tired out. It does not mean improved by the experience of whipping.

"Nekkid as a jaybird" means stark naked. But jays are never naked, so this is inexplicable.

"Raining sideways": "It was raining to beat the band."

"Gullywasher": "It was raining like a cow pissin' on a flat rock."

"He thought he'd died and gone to heaven."= He believed himself extremely successful.

"Hunkered down": having taken shelter

"They flat whipped us": They completely whipped us. "Flat" is an intensifier.

"Well, I'll be" is an expression of mild amazement.

"Fandangled" = complicated, needlessly complex

"A New York minute" means very quickly. "If they are giving out free tickets, I'll be there in a New York minute."

"Persnickety" = fussy, overly particular

"A country mile" is a phrase meaning a great distance, or simply a lot. "They lost the game by a country mile."

"A fur piece" is a great distance. "Hit's a fur piece from here." A fur piece is less than a country mile.

"In high cotton" = a good condition, a privileged state of being. Picking high cotton was easier than bending down to pick the bolls.

"He ain't right" means he is mentally defective. It does not mean he is incorrect.

"Hit don't make no never mind." = "Don't concern yourself with that." ("These are not the droids you are looking for.")

"Peckerwood" = a fool. The American Heritage Dictionary says "peckerwood" is a Southern U.S. term for a woodpecker, which may well be so, but the dominant use in my experience is to name someone a fool.

"Get on down the road" means to move along, make progress, or simply to leave.

"Mighty perticklr" means overly particular, fussy.

"I'll study on it" means, "I will think about it."

"I might could if'n I tried real hard," means that I might be able to do it, if I seriously applied myself to the project.

"Colder than shit" = extremely cold. Which is absurd, because the temperature of feces is 98.6 degrees Fahrenheit.

"How 'bout them apples?" simply means, "What about that?" It can also be a mild request for the listener to comment.

"That ain't much punkin" = not very good.

"A rank stranger" is a complete stranger, an absolute stranger.

"He squoze into that little tiny space." This is an example of a creative past tense. It is unknown to the Oxford English Dictionary, the American Heritage Dictionary, and Webster's Unabridged. "Squeeze" is an example of what philologists call a "weak" verb, meaning a verb which does not change its stem vowel as its tenses change: "I squeeze the tube of paste today. I squeezed it yesterday. I have squeezed it many times."

"He don't know up from down" is a local way of saying that a fellow is dense or stupid.

"That dog don't hunt," means that something is a bad idea, incorrect, false.

"I turned it over in my head," means that I thought about it.

"Hurtin' fer certain" means definitely hurting (as in pain), but more often it means being at a disability or disadvantage.

"Plumb certain" means definitely certain, as correct and straight as a plumb line.

"I can't splain it no other way" occurs often. It is simply an elision of the first syllable.

"What's the dang deal?" = "What's that all about?"

"Dickhead" is a gross term for a fool. But it can also be a mild term of endearment.

"Shut yo' mouf" is a rude way to tell someone to be quiet.

Sayings

SAYINGS EXIST BECAUSE WE USE THEM. THEY CROP UP IN OUR SPEECH, often as a shorthand for thought, but sometimes they are exactly on point. When that happens they are perfectly apt and helpful.

"Until the cows come home" = for a very long, indefinite amount of time. *You can wait until the cows come home, but you'll never see that law passed in this country!* Or again, *My wife talked on the phone with her sister until the cows came home.*

"On the right side of the grass" = still living, as opposed to dead and buried beneath the grass. Often said to indicate one's life is relatively positive, despite difficulties. *No, I didn't have the best day, but at least I woke up on the right side of the grass.*

"Kill two birds with one stone" = To take care of two tasks at the same time. *I might as well kill two birds with one stone and drop off my tax forms while I'm at the mall.*

It is interesting that Germans say the same thing: *Zwei Fliegen mit einer Klappe schlagen.*

"Main strength and awkwardness" = great force; brute force. *They finally got the piano moved into the living room by main strength and awkwardness.* Or again, *Be careful lifting the antique table. It is not a job for main strength and awkwardness.*

"In touch" is a figurative phrase. It means communicating with. *I will get in touch with you tomorrow.*

"Circle back" is similar. *I will check back with you tomorrow. I will circle back then.*

"Haste makes waste" is said when someone is doing something too quickly. *If they hurry, they will waste a lot of time, effort, and materials. Haste makes waste.*

"Out to lunch" = not in touch with the real world; absentminded or uninformed. *Jim's been a bit out to lunch lately, don't you think?*

"It never rains but it pours" is a proverb meaning things happen in large numbers. *Things were going okay, but then I lost my car keys. And then I lost my iphone. And then I fell down and skinned my knee. It never rains but it pours.*

"You can't keep a good man down" means that if people have determination, they will recover from difficulties and be successful. *He'll come through, you'll see. You can't keep a good man down.*

"Close enough for government work" = done just well enough to get by. The thought here is that work for the government is not done with care or pride. *I didn't do the best job mending your shirt, but it's close enough for government work.*

"You know" is a phrase people use when trying to think of what to say next: *Well I just thought, you know, I'd better agree to it, you know. I'm not happy with the situation but, you know, there isn't much I can do about it.*

"One hand washes the other" means all parties benefit from helping each other. *If you feature our company's logo during your campaign, we get a boost in advertising, and you get a bump in campaign funding. One hand washes the other.*

"The devil's own time" refers to something difficult to do *I'm having the devil's own time getting this window open. I think it has been painted shut.*

"A fool is born every minute" is a phrase associated with P. T. Barnum, although there is no evidence that he actually said it.

"Can't hold a candle to" is figurative, meaning a person is unable to measure up to someone else. *Mary can't hold a candle to Ann when it comes to athletics.*

"Bound and determined = extremely motivated. It is often followed by a statement of what is to be done: *I am bound and determined to graduate.* Or again, *I am bound and determined to lose weight.*

"I hear that" is a statement of concurrence. George says, *I'm so glad to be working from home now. I do not miss those morning commutes.* Nancy replies, *I hear that.*

"Slow and steady wins the race" is a proverb. It means by working slowly but constantly, you will succeed better than by working fast for a short while. The proverb comes from Aesop's fable, "The Tortoise and the Hare." *Margaret only had a little time to spend sewing every day, but because she worked steadily, she soon had finished a beautiful quilt.*

"A mind like a steel trap" is a mind capable of grasping information quickly. *David has a mind like a steel trap, so if you give him the instructions, he'll follow them perfectly.*

"If a frog had wings" describes an impossible situation. *We are stuck with what we've got. It would take a miracle now. If a frog had wings . . .*

"Putting on notice" = to warn or alert about something. *Companies are being put on notice that their interest rates will rise in the new year.*

"A stitch in time saves nine" is a proverb meaning that prompt, decisive action now will prevent problems later. *You should consider getting your car repaired now, before you're left stranded on the side of the road. A stitch in time saves nine.*

"The early bird catches the worm." Someone who seizes an opportunity quickly will have the best chance of reaping its benefits. *This market could be very lucrative, but I think it will only be for those who take advantage of it early on. The early bird catches the worm.*

"Out of sight, out of mind" means if you do not see something, you will forget it. *Ever since I moved, none of my friends call me. It's out of sight, out of mind with them, I think.* Or again, *My electric bill got moved to the bottom of the stack, and I forgot all about paying it. Out of sight, out of mind.*

"Slammed" = having an inordinate amount of work suddenly. *Things were quiet in the store until noon, and then we were slammed until closing.*

"Right as rain" = in good order or good health, satisfactory. *He was very ill, but he's right as rain now.*

The allusion is unclear, but it originated in Britain, where rainy weather is a normal fact of life. It was first recorded in 1894.

"The road to hell is paved with good intentions" is a proverb. In 1855 it was published in Henry G. Bohn's *A Hand-book of Proverbs.*

In 1828 it appeared in a London newspaper, where it was called a Portuguese proverb.

An 1811 English version says, "The road to hell is paved with good resolutions."

A 1730 German text stated, "Der Weg zur Höllen sei mit lauter gutem Vorsatz gepflastert."

In 1670, "Hell is full of good meanings and wishes," was published in John Ray's *A Collection of English Proverbs.*

"The proof of the pudding is in the eating." Final results are the only way to judge quality. *Okay, if I did everything right, the engine should start, but the proof of the pudding is in the eating.*

"A pretty penny" = a large amount of money. *By the time the wine is ready for drinking, its value will have risen sufficiently to earn the investor a pretty penny.* Or again, *Buying a home can cost a pretty penny.*

"Clotheshorse." The first meaning is straightforward: a clothes rack for drying clothes.

A second usage is figurative: A person who is always dressed in the latest style.

"Take for granted" means to assume something as true, real, or to be expected: *We took our invitation to the party for granted.* Or again, *The old middle class rose to prominence in the 40s, 50s, and 60s, when economic growth was taken for granted.*

"Ye pass this way but once" may come from Etienne de Grellet, a Quaker missionary, who wrote: *I shall pass this way but once; any good that I can do or any kindness I can show to any human being; let me do it now. Let me not defer nor neglect it, for I shall not pass this way again.*

"If push comes to shove" refers to a crucial point being reached. *If push comes to shove, the Federal Reserve Board will lower the interest rate.* Or again, *They say they support equality, but when push comes to shove they always promote a man.*

"A ton of" = "lots of" It means a very large amount of people or things. *There are still a ton of things we need to get done before the product will be ready to launch.* Or again, *A ton of tourists start pouring into the city just before the festival each year.*

"The whole nine yards" There is no consensus on the origin of this phrase. It may relate to the length of fabric. In the 1800s and early 1900s, cloth was sold in standard lengths of nine yards. The phrase "...she has put the whole nine yards into one shirt" appears in 1855.

A common explanation is that "nine yards" is the cubic measure of a concrete mixer, but because the phrase appeared back in 1855, a concrete mixer is inconsistent with the history of the phrase.

Still, it is possible that people today think of the concrete mixer when they use the phrase.

"All your eggs in one basket" is from an old proverb, and first found in print during the 17th century. It alludes to gathering all the eggs from your hens into one basket. If you drop the basket, you lose all your eggs.

It appears in 1615 in Don Quixote by Miguel de Cervantes: "...to withdraw is not to run away, and to stay is no wise action when there's more reason to fear than to hope; 'tis the part of a wise man to keep himself today for tomorrow, and not venture all his eggs in one basket."

In 1666 it appears in A Common Place of Italian Proverbs and Proverbial Phrases by Giovanni Torriano.

"Keep the wolf from the door" means to ward off starvation or insolvency. Based on lupine ravenousness, it dates from the sixteenth century in John Heywood's Proverbs (1546).

It had become a cliché by 1800.

"Don't jinx yourself" is grounded in superstition, the belief being that a jinx is a curse or attribute attracting bad luck. It has been used this way since the 17th century.

In the 21st century, the suggestion that a ship might be "jinxed" was used to describe two cruise liners after misfortunes.

Germans have a roundabout way of getting to the same thing. They say a person should not "paint the devil on the wall." "Den Teufel nicht auf die Wand malen."

To speak of a bad outcome brings it on.

"It speaks well/poorly" is chiefly used in the U.S. *It speaks well for the company that it donates so much money to local charities.* Or, alternatively, *These test results speak poorly for our school system.*

"Going south" means "to decline." It comes from maps, where north is up and south is down. This begs the question, what about Australians?

"All she wrote" is informal, expressing that there is nothing more that can be said on the topic. *All you have to do to fire the gun is point it and shoot it. That's all she wrote.*

"Necessity is the mother of invention" has an ancient history. Aesop, 620–564, tells of a thirsty crow coming upon a pitcher with water at the bottom. The crow wants to drink the water, but it cannot reach the water with its beak. It tries to push the pitcher over but fails.

It then drops in pebbles one by one until the water rises to the top of the pitcher, allowing him to drink.

"Weak as water" means lacking physical strength or vigor. *You'll always be weak as water if you stay inside playing video games.*

"A hard hill to climb" is used figuratively to express that a task is difficult.

"Going to town" means to act with energy or enthusiasm. *We only planned to paint one room, but we went to town and painted the whole upstairs.*

"Hung the moon" is used to speak of someone as extraordinary. *Your sister adores you. She thinks you hung the moon.*

"A godsend" is a desirable or needed thing that comes unexpectedly. *The widespread rain was a godsend for farmers.*

"Happy camper" = an individual pleased with the circumstances; a contented person. But, in the negative, *If our business falls off 40%, we are not going to be happy campers.*

"A bird in the hand is worth two in the bush" means it is better to hold on to what you have than to risk losing it going for something more.

"All who wander are not lost" and "Not all who wander are lost' come most recently from Tolkien's Fellowship of the Ring, "The Riddle of Strider."

But of course, the saying can have philosophical significance for any speaker.

"Third time's a charm." Two efforts have already failed, but perhaps the third will be successful.

"Pushing the envelope" means going beyond normal limits. The saying comes from flight testing in the 1960s, where the envelope was the limit of safe performance. By the 1980s the expression was used figuratively, and so widely that it became a cliché.

"Betimes" means early. *He was up betimes doing his lessons.*

"Fard" is a relatively uncommon little word. When it is encountered these days it is often in participle form, "farding."

Fard was borrowed from Anglo-French from the verb *farder*. It first appeared in English in the mid-1400s. It is of Germanic origin and is akin to the Old High German word *faro,* meaning "colored."

"If it ain't broke, don't fix it" is an expression meaning that if something is producing the required results, don't tinker with it. Focus instead on what's working well and ride the momentum to the upside.

The expression originates with Thomas Bertram Lance, the Director of the Office of Management and Budget in the Carter administration. The newsletter of the US Chamber of Commerce, *Nation's Business,* quoted Lance as saying the government could save billions of dollars by following the principle.

"The perfect is the enemy of the good" means insisting on perfection often prevents implementation of good improvements.

The "Pareto principle" explains this numerically: It takes 20% of the full time for a task to do 80% of it.

But, to complete the 20% which remains uncompleted takes 80% of the effort.

"You could hang meat in here" means that it is frigid where the speaker is. The reason for the cold is to keep the meat from spoiling. *That classroom is so cold you could hang meat in there.*

"There's more than one way to skin a cat" means there are many ways to accomplish the same end. In 1854 it appeared in *Way down East; Portraitures of Yankee Life* by Seba Smith.

"A bridge too far" is an act or plan whose ambition overreaches its capability, resulting in difficulty or failure.

It is taken from *A Bridge Too Far* by Cornelius Ryan (1974), detailing the Allies' failed attempts to capture German-controlled bridges in the Netherlands during World War II's Operation Market Garden.

"Too far out over your skis" = "Don't get ahead of yourself." Used as a suggestion to mean, "Take it one step at a time."

"Don't poke the bear" means, do not irritate or bother someone, when doing so carries an obvious risk. *Uncle Ned has finally stopped railing against the Cleveland* Browns, *so you better not poke the bear and get him going again!*

"Humble pie" is figurative, referring to humiliation, usually in the form of a forced submission, apology, or retraction. It is often used in the phrase "eat humble pie." Humbles are the entrails of a deer, poor food.

"Up to snuff" means "satisfactory." The origins of the saying are confused, but are all related to powdered tobacco inhaled up the nose.

"Air in a jug" *I wouldn't give Yale University air in a jug."*

More commonly it is used for a person: "I wouldn't give him air in a jug. I think that little of him."

"Come a cropper" means "take a heavy fall" To suffer a collapse, crash, defeat, failure, fizzle, nonachievement, nonsuccess.

"Since God was a child" = for a long time right up to the present. *I haven't heard from you since God was a child.*

"Like mushrooms after a spring rain" means something has appeared unexpectedly in great abundance.

"To hector" means to bully someone. The original Hector of Homer's *Iliad* was not a bully. He was the eldest son of King Priam of Troy, a model soldier, son, father, and friend. He was the champion of the Trojan army until killed by the Greek hero Achilles.

How did a Trojan paragon become today's generic synonym of *bully*?

That pejorative English use comes from gangs of street toughs who roamed London in the 17th century and called themselves "Hectors."

They believed they were gallant young blades, but to normal people they were swaggering bullies who intimidated passersby and vandalized property.

By 1660, "hector" was being used as a noun for the sort of blustering braggarts who populated those gangs, and as a verb as well.

In the *Iliad,* the counterpart to Hector was Nestor, the eldest of the Greek leaders in the Trojan War.

He had been a great warrior as a young man, but in the *Iliad* is noted chiefly for his wisdom and talkativeness, both of which increased as he aged.

These days, a nestor is not necessarily long-winded, but merely wise and generous with his advice.

A second meaning of a nestor today is a patriarch or leader in a field.

"It is high time" means something is overdue to happen. In German, the phrase is *"höchste Zeit"*: *"Es ist ja höchste Zeit, dass du nach Hause kommst."*

"Thou shalt not muzzle the ox that treads thy grain" is from Deuteronomy 25:4. The point is that the laborer is worthy of his hire.

"Hand over fist" = rapidly, quickly. This is believed to come from a sailor's hauling in of a line rapidly, hand over hand.

"Cry uncle," is a call for another to submit, or cry for mercy. It appears variously as *say uncle!, cry uncle!,* or *holler uncle!* First recorded in print in the twentieth century.

"Like a redheaded stepchild" means out of the gene pool, out of place, a child who is obviously not your own. This child is treated worse than other children in the family.

Particularly in noble circles, the presence of a stepchild or illegitimate child posed a threat to inheritance. Shakespeare used the illegitimate child: Edmund the Bastard in *King Lear* and John the Bastard in *Much Ado About Nothing*.

Snow White and *Cinderella* stress conflict between stepparents and stepchildren.

"To beat the band" = extremely: "It was raining to beat the band."

"Going nowhere fast" = "spinning your wheels" = "What you are engaged in is futile."

"I didn't know him from Adam's off ox." An "off ox" is the draft animal in a team situated on the right, farthest from the driver. The driver places the most experienced draft animal closest to his guiding leads, hoping the off ox will simply follow what the lead animal does.

The off ox often does not have the best footing in a situation, and may stumble.

Also, the off ox is not as prized as the near ox, and the idiom "poor as Adam's off ox" did not emerge into popular culture until Bill Clinton used it in the 1990s.

"My stomach thinks my throat's cut" means simply, "I am very hungry."

"Damn straight" = "absolutely"

"Quiet as a mouse" = very quiet. *And all through the house, not a creature was stirring, not even a mouse.*

"Deaf as a post" dates from the 16th century. It is first recorded in *The Comedye of Acolastus* (1540) by John Palsgrave.

"The cat's meow" = the epitome, perfection. *She thought she was just the cat's meow.* Or again, *I really like that car; it's the cat's meow.*

"Silly goose" refers to a person who acts in a foolish, somewhat comical way. This term originates from several sources. Brewer's *Dictionary of Phrase and Fable* states, "A foolish or ignorant person is called a goose because of the alleged stupidity of this bird."

"Couldn't hear yourself think" *There was so much noise I was unable to form thoughts.*

"Dead to rights" The *Dictionary of Clichés* by Christine Ammer says it means "being absolutely without doubt; also, red-handed, in the act of doing something."

The term originated in the mid-nineteenth century and was used mostly with criminal activity.

In 1859 George Washington Marsell defined it in his *Vocabulum* (also called *The Rogue's Lexicon*) as "positively guilty with no way of getting clear."

"Standoffish" is said of a detached or reserved person, for example a person who avoids eye contact and doesn't talk with people in a group setting.

"Dead as a doornail" = definitely deceased

Old Marley was as dead as a door-nail. Mind! I don't mean to say that I know, of my own knowledge, what there is particularly dead about a door-nail. I might have been inclined, myself, to regard a coffin-nail as the deadest piece of ironmongery in the trade. But the wisdom of our ancestors is in the simile; and my unhallowed hands shall not disturb it, or the Country's done for. You will therefore permit me to repeat, emphatically, that Marley was as dead as a door-nail.

"Sweet as pie" = Particularly sweet, friendly, or kindly. *The kids may be sweet as pie right now, but they can be little terrors when they want to be.*

"Suck-up"= ass kisser, brown noser. *He was a suck-up.*

"A stick in the mud" is a person who is slow, old-fashioned, unprogressive; an old fogey.

"Spoilsport" = One who mars the pleasure of others. Someone who puts an end to others' fun.

"Had me/got me by the short hairs" = To acquire complete control, dominance, or power over someone, especially in a difficult or awkward situation.

"Frightened/scared me out of my wits" means "afraid, fearful, nervous, panicky, agitated, alarmed, worried, intimidated."

"At my wits' end" means out of options, in a hopeless state. *I was so worried and confused I did not know what to do next.*

"Topsy-turvy" = in utter confusion or disorder; also, with the top or head downward. Upside down.

"Sad sack" = a blundering, inept person

Sad Sack was an American World War II comic strip character of George Baker, who depicted an otherwise unnamed, lowly private experiencing absurdities and humiliations in military life.

The title was a euphemistic shortening of the military slang "sad sack of shit."

"I did it on a lark" means to do something on a whim or just for fun. *On a lark we diverted our journey from Rome to Amsterdam.*

A lark, in British slang, is a gag or a joke. The phrase "on a lark" is then something done as a joke.

"What the Sam Hill!" is American English slang. It is a minced oath for "the devil" or "hell." ("What in the Sam Hill is that?")

According to the Oxford English Dictionary it is of unknown origin. Etymologist Michael Quinion dates the expression to the late 1830s. It is a simple bowdlerization.

To "bowdlerize" is to remove material that is considered offensive or objectionable. Thomas Bowdler, 1754-1825, was an English physician who published *The Family Shakespeare*, an expurgated edition of Shakespeare's plays, more appropriate, Bowdler felt, for women and children.

"Shot my wad" comes from the days of musket guns, where a wad (strips of cloth) was packed down the barrel to create a seal between the gunpowder and the bullet, increasing the internal pressure when the gunpowder fired, and thus speeding the bullet.

Today, it can mean to lose or spend all one's money. *My Las Vegas trip was short lived. I shot my wad at poker in the first two hours!*

"Hokum" is pretentious nonsense. Also called "bunkum." It is something apparently legitimate but actually untrue or insincere; nonsense.

"Pull my leg" = to tease or fool someone; to trick someone in a humorous way.

"He was real keerful on the chance they was a snake the other side of the log."

"Purt near" = pretty near; almost

"That wadn't bad." = "That was pretty good." Here the negative is used to yield a positive.

"Gwine to do": "I'm gwine to do that, first chanct I git." I intend to do that as soon as possible.

"Crooked as a snake" = extremely dishonest

"Roon" = ruin. Roon is used as a verb, never as a noun. "If'n you put your sharp knives in the dishwasher, it'll roon 'em."

"Blarey" = "blurry" This word may be a combination of "glare" and "blur."

"That's just mizzibl." = "That is simply miserable, really too bad, regrettable."

"I'm gone kick yo' ass." The word "gone" here rhymes with tone and moan. The "gone" here means "going to."

"As slick as owl grease" = extremely excellent. The expression is popular throughout the South. "Alcalde oil is as slick as owl grease" was cited in Texas newspapers in 1894.

"Fast as greased lightning" means extremely fast.

"Crazy as a jaybird" = extremely crazy

"Right smuck in the middle" "Smuck" here is used alternatively to "smack." Both the words mean "exactly in the middle."

"Getting nowhere fast" = making no progress, spinning your wheels in the sand.

"They seen you comin'" means, "They knew they could take advantage of you, so they fleeced you."

To "fleece someone" is to take his money. An example is the "fish" in a poker game, someone invited because he is known to lose.

"Not worth a tinker's damn" There is disagreement here. Some claim it is *tinker's dam* while others say it should be *tinker's damn*.

A tinker travels, repairing small things like utensils.

An1877 definition of *tinker's dam* stated that a tinker's dam was a piece of doughy material used to hold metal in place when repairing it.

The idea was that this material was worthless once the repair was complete, since it couldn't be reused and could serve no alternative purpose.

"All swole up": "He was all swole up from them bee stangs." *Swole* has existed in English since at least the early 1900s. It is used as another word for *swelled* or *swollen*.

"Out of kilter" = askew. "There's something out of kilter here."

"Hellacious" = extremely, awfully. *This is hellacious good chili.*

"Tarnation" = damnation, hell. Usually with "in." "What in tarnation were you thinking?"

"Gumpshun" = gumption = courage

"Cattywampus" = crooked, out of kilter

"Piss poor" = extremely poor

"A pot to piss in": *He was so poor he didn't have a pot to piss in.* This probably refers to the times of chamber pots.

"You're pissin' out." This means, "You are giving up, have lost your motivation, you are tired."

It does not mean to urinate in the outward direction.

"Piss off!" is an exclamation meaning, "Get lost, go away, don't bother me."

"Pissed off": To be "pissed off" is a condition of vexation.

"Skeezix": an imaginary body part. *Be careful or you'll break your skeezix.*

"Summer's": *It's here summer's.* = "It is here somewhere."

It does not mean that something is present in the summer.

"A piece of work": a fool, a person out of step. *He is a piece of work.*

"A mort of trouble" = a lot of trouble. "Mort" means a great number. It was first used as such in 1694.

"Sucking wind" = accomplishing nothing, being out of luck. This probably comes from the anatomical pneumothorax.

"Fit to be tied": frustrated, upset, out of options

"Fine as frog's hair" means extremely excellent. It has nothing to do with the thinness of the filaments.

"Let's nail it." = "Let's do it, let's get it done."

"Cold beer" of course means what it says. But in East Tennessee it is pronounced as one word, accenting the first syllable: *Please bring me a **cold**beer.*

"At all" is like "cold beer." It is a matter of pronunciation. The way to say it in East Tennessee is **ay**tall. *They ain't no hope a' figgerin' this out **ay**tall.* The emphasis must be on the first syllable.

"Damn fool" is pronounced the same way as "**Cold**beer": The emphasis must be on the first syllable. *He is just a **damn**fool.*

"Dogwood winter"

Our ancestors relied on the signs of nature around them. Dogwood Wintercomes during late April or early May, around the time dogwood trees start blooming. Farmers knew it wasn't safe to plant crops until after the dogwoods bloomed.

"Blackberry winter" is a cold snap in late spring when blackberries are in bloom.

Centuries of observing nature's phenomena taught important lessons, when some days from March into May are summer-like and others threaten frost.

Today's scientists call this phenology, which is the study of cyclic and seasonal natural phenomena. In the days before the National Weather Service, when most Tennesseans still worked on the farm, reading weather behavior from the signs was a survival skill. Farmers depended on folk wisdom to plant their crops and gardens.

"Scientific" farmers also kept journals noting the weather and other phenomena, allowing them to increase their harvest and income. One of the earliest such farming journals in the Tennessee Historical Society's collections belonged to John Sevier, first governor of Tennessee.

In terse notes, Sevier remarked on what would have been dogwood winter:

[April 1795] Sun. 20 Wintry & cool Mr. Sherrill & son Wm. Dined.

The next April, in 1796, Sevier observed:

Sun. 24 very sultry & cloudy. Mon. 25 Knox. Court begun. Tues. 26 Fine rain, and rained in night. Mrs. Smith was here--Wed. 27 very cloudy in the morning. Cool in the night river raised also. Thur 28 is very cool for the season. Fros. Fry. 29 light Frost. Sat. 30 some warmer.

Through such observations year after year, farmers knew to wait before planting cold-sensitive crops such as corn, tobacco, and cotton. The knowledge could save them from disastrous losses and increase the yields from their labor.

"Daggone" = "dadgummit," a mild curse.

"Cut some slack" denotes allowing someone more latitude or freedom than usual.

"With my teeth in my mouth" means, "I was doing nothing. I was useless." For example, *"I was standing there with my teeth in my mouth when I could have helped Nancy start her car."*

"Freezing my ass off" means "I am really cold." This is said although it could not literally happen. It is figurative speech.

"My ass is in a crack." = "I am in trouble." Alternatively, "I have made a mistake."

"Cruisin' for a bruisin'" = "You are looking for trouble," or alternatively, "You had better watch out."

"Poot" = "phooey" As a noun, poot has two meanings: a mild expression of disgust and the passing of gas. As a verb it means to pass gas.

"Shinola" is a brand of shoe polish. With brown Shinola, *You don't know from Shinola. = You don't know from shit. = You know nothing.*

"I can't see from Shinola." = "I can't see anything." The visual hindrance is severe. *I was at the corner. There were bushes to my left blocking the view. I couldn't see from Shinola.*

"He don't know from squat." = "He don't know from Shinola. = "He don't know poot."

"Big honking"= "large" *There was a big honking log in my way.*

"Tits on a boar hog" is said to refer to something useless.

"Shit out of luck" means, "You have no further options." Often abbreviated to the acronym SOL. *Well, Robert, at this point you are SOL.*

"Root hog or die" refers to self-reliance. It dates at least to the early 1800s. It comes from the practice of turning pigs loose in the woods to fend for themselves.

"Running like a chicken with its head cut off" refers to acting in a frenzied manner, distractedly, crazily. *She ran around the station looking for her lost bag like a chicken with its head cut off.* The body of a decapitated chicken totters about crazily for a while.

"Sumbitch" = "son of a bitch." It does not mean "some bitch."

"Pissant" is an inferior and bothersome person. The word comes from the fourteenth century "pismire," meaning "urinating ant." The odor of formic acid is a characteristic of an ant hill.

"They, law" = "How about that?"

"Let me tell you" means what it says in normal English: "Allow me to narrate something to you." But it also means "I agree." *Alabama is going to beat Tennessee this year.* Response: *Let me tell you.*

"Kindly" = "kind of" *"Hit's kindly bright in here,"* means "It is rather bright in here."

Eternal life

THE GOSPEL OF JOHN HAS MANY REFERENCES TO ETERNAL LIFE, THE most famous being John 3:16:

> *For God so loved the world, that he gave his only Son, that whoever believes in him should not perish but have eternal life.*

John 3:36 states,

> *Whoever believes in the Son has eternal life; whoever does not obey the Son shall not see life, but the wrath of God remains on him.*

At John 4:14, Jesus tells the Samaritan woman at the well that,

> *Everyone who drinks of this water will be thirsty again, but whoever drinks of the water that I will give him will never be thirsty again. The water that I will give him will become in him a spring of water welling up to eternal life.*

At John 5:24, Jesus states,

> *whoever hears my word and believes him who sent me has eternal life. He does not come into judgment, but has passed from death to life.*

In John 6:27, Jesus,

> *Do not work for the food that perishes, but for the food that endures to eternal life, which the Son of Man will give to you.*

At John 6:51 we are told,

> *I am the living bread that came down from heaven. If anyone eats of this bread, he will live forever. And the bread that I will give for the life of the world is my flesh.*

At John 6:54 ff we read:

> *Whoever feeds on my flesh and drinks my blood has eternal life, and I will raise him up on the last day. For my flesh is true food, and my blood is true drink. Whoever feeds on my flesh and drinks my blood abides in me, and I in him. As the living Father sent me, and I live because of the Father, so whoever feeds on me, he also will live because of me. This is the bread that came down from heaven, not like the bread the fathers ate, and died. Whoever feeds on this bread will live forever.*

Peter

It is Peter--the repeatedly bumbling Peter who denied Christ three times--it is this man who in the book of Acts rises to lead the nascent church.

This mature Peter defies those who crucified Christ. He says what must be done: repent and be baptized. He knows who his enemies are, and he is ready for them.

Peter earlier was bumbling, impetuous, a magnet for mistakes. And then he became the rock upon which the church is built. What happened? Two things. Two outpourings of the holy spirit: the one vast outpouring at Pentecost, but also an earlier one: After the crucifixion, Christ appears to the disciples (John 20:21):

> *Jesus said to them again, "Peace be with you. As the Father has sent me, even so I am sending you."*
>
> *And when he had said this, he breathed on them and said to them, "Receive the Holy Spirit. If you forgive the sins of any, they are forgiven them; if you withhold forgiveness from any, it is withheld."*

The 23d Psalm

The LORD is my shepherd; I shall not want.

He maketh me to lie down in green pastures: he leadeth me beside the still waters.

He restoreth my soul: he leadeth me in the paths of righteousness for his name's sake.

Yea, though I walk through the valley of the shadow of death, I will fear no evil: for thou art with me; thy rod and thy staff they comfort me.

Thou preparest a table before me in the presence of mine enemies: thou anointest my head with oil; my cup runneth over.

Surely goodness and mercy shall follow me all the days of my life: and I will dwell in the house of the LORD for ever.

IN 2021 I WROTE ABOUT THE SHEPHERD AND HIS FLOCK, A THEME IN both the old and new testaments. The 23d Psalm is also about the shepherd and his flock. This time it is a flock of one, the speaker of the psalm. The comfortable and familiar language begins,

The Lord is my shepherd; I shall not want.

That very first word announces monotheism. It is the Lord. Only one Lord, not the multiple gods of the Greeks and the Romans, not the multiple gods of the Egyptians or the Incas. One God, the Lord.

What about this monotheistic God? "*The Lord is.*" The Lord simply is. We live and breathe and have our being in this one God.

"*The Lord is my shepherd,*" we read. The take-away word here is "my." The Lord ministers to me. Even to me, even to humble me. My Lord is personal. He is taking care of me. He is addressing my needs. He does this by being my shepherd, my caregiver, my protector.

We are so accustomed to the King James 1611 text that the whole psalm can simply flow over us in a rush of beauty. This is good, but there are individual building blocks in this beauty.

This God who is my shepherd,

> *maketh me to lie down in green pastures: he leadeth me beside the still waters.*

This God, my shepherd, gives me peace. He makes me calm. He takes away my worries. He builds me up. He replenishes my innermost being, my soul:

> *He restoreth my soul: he leadeth me in the paths of righteousness for his name's sake.*

He leads me to correct behavior for the glory of God.

The speaker is not to fear. Even as the sheep and the speaker were protected, bedded down, given water to drink, the speaker is now protected even from death:

> *Yea, though I walk through the valley of the shadow of death, I will fear no evil, for thou art with me.*

> *Thy rod and thy staff they comfort me.*

His enemies are nothing to him. He defies them with God's help:

> *Thou preparest a table before me in the presence of mine enemies:*
> *thou anointest my head with oil; my cup runneth over.*

God has demonstrated his love. He will follow his paths. He is protected, led. He lives and acts for the glory of God's name, walking in the paths of righteousness.

> *Surely goodness and mercy shall follow me all the days of my life: and I will dwell in the house of the LORD forever.*

John chapter 10 gives us Christ's words: "*I am the good shepherd. I know my own, and my own know me, just as the Father knows me and I know the Father; and I lay down my life for the sheep.*"

School

SCHOOL, 1949-1952

The boy threw up on the way to school,
Regularly,
A matter of course,
Compass-setting.
The stink of decomposing plankton
Would rise into his blowholes,
And make his bright eyes water,
Make the sidewalk swim.
His almost hairless body, half-formed,
Wet cetacean eyes casting about,
Sought protection, not ritual heaves,
Not emesis on neighborhood lawns.

His mother protected him when she could,
Let him swim in her shadow,
Helped him feed, hid him
When she herself was not in danger,
The denouncéd whore, the common slut,
The bright-eyed nurse.

He scraped his way along the sidewalks
Thinking six times nine, four times three,
Thinking bile-tinged thoughts.
He thought of the school cafeteria, steaming,
Waiting, windows fogged,
A place that sometimes had no food for whales.
He thought of home and crashing waves,
The leaping thrashing father,

Up, up into bright air,
Leaping high and falling back into the sea,
Killing what lay below him,
Denouncing the whore.

He wondered how it could be
That at home only she loved him,
Only his mother,
While at school many, many loved him.
Even the ladies in the cafeteria,
Even on the days
When there was no food for whales.

He thought of children, tiered and glowing,
Standing on stair steps reaching
All the way to heaven,
Reaching so high the air was thin and shimmering
Where the oldest stood, singing,
Singing in the school's foyer,
Singing Oh, little town,
Singing with no fear of megaliths
Falling, white-crusted, waves driven asunder,
Gulls sent screaming,
Their wingtips slapping foam.

He thought of his teacher who loved him,
Who loved his gray skin,
His smooth gray skin,
Who gave him stamps and stars.
At night, rising to breathe,
He saw her stars among the stars,
Her stamped cat shapes upon the constellations.
At night, rising to breathe,
He knew he wanted to live in school,
Wanted to breathe the dust of tempera paints
And construction paper forever,

Far from falling fear,
Far from barnacled screams.
He knew he wanted to live, and live, and live,
Without bile, without flukes,
Beyond the horizon, among the stars.

Written by Bill Swann, and published in *Homeworks* (University of Tennessee Press, 1986)

Kirksey believed certain poems could not be forgotten

At least parts of them. That is, once you heard them, they just stuck with you. Whether because of meter, image, or the simple flow of sound, there it was.

Poe's "Raven":

> Once upon a midnight dreary, while I pondered, weak
> and weary,
> Over many a quaint and curious volume of forgotten
> lore—
> While I nodded, nearly napping, suddenly there came
> a tapping,
> As of some one gently rapping, rapping at my chamber
> door.
> "'Tis some visitor," I muttered, "tapping at my chamber
> door—
> Only this and nothing more."

Tennyson's "Tithonus":

> The woods decay, the woods decay and fall,
> The vapours weep their burthen to the ground,
> Man comes and tills the field and lies beneath,
> And after many a summer dies the swan.

Sidney Lanier's "Marshes of Glynn":

> Glooms of the live-oaks, beautiful-braided and woven
> With intricate shades of the vines that myriad-cloven
> Clamber the forks of the multiform boughs . . .

Hawthorne's _"Evangeline"_:

> This is the forest primeval. The murmuring pines and
> the hemlocks,
> Bearded with moss, and in garments green, indistinct
> in the twilight,
> Stand like Druids of eld, with voices sad and prophetic,
> Stand like harpers hoar, with beards that rest on their
> bosoms.

Heine's _"Lorelei"_:

> _Ich weiss nicht, was soll es bedeuten,_
> _Dass ich so traurig bin;_
> _Ein Märchen aus alten Zeiten,_
> _Das kommt mir nicht aus dem Sinn._

> I don't know what it means
> That I am so sad
> A legend of bygone days
> That I cannot keep out of my mind.

When he killed the Mudjokevis*

When he killed the mudjokevis,
Of the skin he made him mittens,
Made them with the fur side inside,
Made them with the skin side outside.
He to get the cold side outside,
Put the warm side fur side inside.
He to get the warm side inside,
Put the cold side skin side outside.
That's why he put the skin side outside,
Why he put the fur side inside,
Why he turned it inside outside.

*If my doggerel here reminds you of Henry Wadsworth Longfellow's hugely successful *Hiawatha* (1855), good for you.

A Song of the North

I WROTE THIS PIECE IN TROCHAIC TETRAMETER, A METER WHICH JUST pounds along. Many know the meter from Poe's "Raven." A trochee is two syllables, with the accent on the first syllable. Put four of those trochees together and you have tetrameter.

This piece talks about my four great fishing buddies, and our many trips to Kishkutena Lake and Loonhaunt Lake in Northwest Ontario. We always landed in International Falls, Minnesota ("the land of Delta)" and drove across the border to Nestor Falls, Ontario. Then we flew by float plane to one of the two lakes. We might transfer to the other lake during our stay.

The references to UMCO (the Upper Minnesota corporation) refer to the wonderful and valuable aluminum tackle boxes John Harber gave us all. But they also refer to the (completely invented) mythology of the UMCO corporation.

Harber and I insisted that Steve Sharp aspired to know the UMCO mythology and that he wanted to attend UMCO functions (which Harber and I say we attended), and from which Steve Sharp was excluded.

Dramatis personae:

--John Harber ("priest most high to noble UMCO"), who patiently taught your author to fish, despite your author's many bird nests (snarls of fishing line).

--Bob Swan ("Swanfly," "Apple Chopper," "He with wand of slender girth"), who tried fly fishing on the two lakes, Kishkutena and

Loonhaunt, to no avail. Bob also restored a fly rod your author inherited from his father.

--Sterling Swann ("Swanling," "He who wasteth not a morsel," "Swanee's brother"), who was taught to fish by your author. And who has become an excellent fisherman.

--Steve Sharp ("Sharplet," "He who made the loathsome image"), who put a four-foot wide cardboard bowtie on the front of his boat (the loathsome image), believing that it would increase his fishing luck. It did not. Steve is the only one of the five who always did the hard lifting and carrying, and always was of good cheer.

--Bill Swann ("Swanee,") your author

--The Wendigo ("Wendy"), see footnote one below. A creature with "burning feet of fire," a "damn moss eater," known to the Cree and other Indians, and universally feared. The Wendigo is able to capture men, carry them up high, and drop them far from the pick-up place. Those who have "seen the Wendigo" go insane.

> *These are tales men tell by firelight,*
> *tell on Loonhaunt's shining waters,*
> *tell when dark night falls upon them,*
> *when the Wendy[1] haunts the trees.*
> *These are tales of Kish-ku-tee-nah,*
> *of the big lake's roaring wind storms,*
> *of the quiet of the evenings*
> *when the Wendy haunts the trees.*
> *These are Tales of men a-questing,*
> *tales of men who seek the walleye,*
> *seek him in the depths of Loonhaunt,*
> *seek the musky where he bides.*

[1] "The Wendigo," by Algernon Blackwood, 1910

Hear now tales of five Intrepids.
Know them jointly, know them singly.
Hear of Harber, mighty Harber,
priest most high to noble UMCO,
high priest to the water-ruler,
ruler of the lakesea waters.

The five Intrepids

Sharplet, Swanfly, Harber, Swanee,
these with Swanling make the five,
make the five who ply these waters,
make the five who know the northwoods,
make the five who fear not Wendy,
men who fear not feet of fire.

These are men who come a-winging,
landing bounce-foot on the waters,
on the shining lakesea waters,
Kish-ku-tee-nah, Loonhaunt mighty,
shining, dancing lakesea waters.

> *Should you ask me, whence these stories?*
> *Whence these legends and traditions?*
> *Whence the odors of the forest*
> *with the dew and damp of meadows,*
> *with the curling smoke of pinewood,*
> *split by Sharplet, daily done?*
> *I should answer, I should tell you,*
> *"From the forests and the prairies,*
> *from the great lakes of the Northland,*
> *from the land of Kish-ku-tee-nah,*
> *from the land of Loonhaunt mighty,*
> *from that land our northern home."*

Where the Harber brought his men

Learn how Harber came far northward,
brought these questers, gave them tokens,
gave them tokens made of metal,
made of wondrous Al-u-min-um,
bought them tokens--praise his name!--
gave them tokens from the UMCO,
offerings humble, some with problems.

Learn how Harber, priest to UMCO,
brought the Swanee to these waters,
taught the Swanee how to thrive there,
took from Swanee mighty birds' nests,
showed him reed beds, taught him casting,
taught him all the Swanee needed,
taught the Swanee skills abounding,
that the Swanee pass them on.

Hear of Swanling, Swanee's brother,
mighty pupil, friend to all.
Hear how Swanling learned the fish-skills,
learned them from his Swanee brother.
Hear how Swanling climbed the pine trees,
climbed the cedars o'er and o'er,
e're he learned the art of casting,
fouling not upon the shore.

Hear of Swanfly, patient quester,
he with wand of slender girth,
he abjuring oft the spin rod,
prizing labor, failing much.
He well knowing how the wind doth
skew his offering to the smallmouth,
he still questing with the slimness,
knowing virtue lives in pain.

Hear the tales of Sharplet heavy,
often forced to fish alone.
He who smiling motored onward,
catching nothing, not downcast.
Hear how Sharplet daily fueled them,
carried gas cans down the dock,
fueled the questers in their boats,
he not shirking from the labor,
he so strong of arm and mirth.

Hear of Moose Pass, hear of White Rocks,
impervious horrors, leeward shore.
Hear of plastics sadly grounded,
lost forever, sadly given,
left to weather 'neath the waters,
winter-over, lonely, lonesome,
ne'er again in UMCO boxes,
warm and tidy, row on row.

How the Swanling stocked the larder

In the land of Minn-ah-so-tah,
in the land where grounds the Delta,
provender did Swanling find there,
loaded carts with costly plunder,
loaded carts with vittles wholesome,
loaded carts with cheese and bratwurst.

Nay, he sought not just nutrition,
nay, he bought for Sharplet cookies,
donuts sought he for the Swanfly.
There he found the brock-oh-lee-ah,
there he found the salad makings,
there he bought the reams of paper--
towels, napkins, plates for serving--
for he knew the needs of Swanee,

he who serves the neatness god.
There he bought the spray of Clorox,
spray of Windex, myrrh of beauty,
there he served his older brother,
mighty Swanee, fishing mentor.

Hear of pasteboards, hear of wagers.
Hear of lies most boldly spoken.
Hear of men's prevarications,
pennies lost, and pennies gained.

How the Swanfly chopped the apples

At behest of Mighty Harber,
priest of UMCO, faithful mentor,
Swanfly duly chopped the apples,
peeled the apples--lo, the many!--
at behest of Mighty Harber,
doing so and so, just so,
tiring not from boring labor,
soldiering onward in his duty.

Hear how Kandyce, far-off Kandyce,
priestess adjunct to the Harber,
writ the 'structions for the apples,
lest the Harber priest-man foul them,
foul the plans so carefully made.
Lest the Harber make a bird's nest
of the makings duly written,
bought by Swanling, land of Delta.

Yea, the Swanling bought store pastry,
trusting not the Harber's skills.
Swanling bought not flour nor leav'ning,
bought not powder, nay, not soda,
those things needful for true pastry.

Nay, he bought not noble makings.
He bought store-made, plebe-man pastry,
trusting not the Harber's skills.

How the Harber gave them boxes

Hear how Harber spared not lucre,
spared not effort, spared not time.
Hear how Harber, mighty priest-man,
sought out online gifts of glory.
Hear how Harber, mighty Harber,
gave them trappings of his bounty,
gave them boxes for to fill them,
fill them with the costly plastics,
plastics for the shining waters,
for the shining lakesea waters.

Hear how Harber bought not leeches,
knowing live bait far beneath him.
Hear how Harber trolled the plastics,
boring Swanee and his brother,
boring Swanfly, boring Sharplet,
boring even fearsome Wendy
watching them from in the trees.

Hear how Harber trolled the depth line,
speaking oft of "fish suspended."
This he did on Kish-ku-tee-nah,
Did for long hours, catching nothing.
Swanee weeping, Swanee moaning.
Did he then express some pity?
Save his friend from awesome sunburn?
Nay, he did not! Trolled for hours,
in the hot sun, in the wind.
Mighty was the quest he followed,
fruitless was the end he gained.

Booty gained he? Booty nary.
Fruitless was the end he gained.

How the Harber was redeemed

Then came he to Loonhaunt mighty,
Loonhaunt, home of lake trout hungry,
Loonhaunt of the great sea waters,
Loonhaunt of the reed beds fruitful.
There did Harber, mighty Harber,
priest to UMCO, show his grandeur.
There did Harber prove his instinct.
There did Harber triumph worthy,
show the Swanee fruits of labor,
teach the Swanee not to doubt him,
teach the Swanee e'er to trust him,
trust him on the Loonhaunt waters.

How Swanfly killed baby pike

"'Ware the Swanfly!" cried the pikelets,
"Here again! Oh woe! Oh woe!
He with hatchet, loathsome deadly,
he will kill us once again!"
And 'twas true. The Swanfly deadly
swung his hatchet on the babies,
soon's they took his presentation.
For this grimness Harber praised him,
He not liking small pikes either.
He yclept them "stinking slime-heads,"
this and more names foul, so foul.
Swanfly brought his little hatchet
for to kill the pike who grieved him,
for to kill the little fellows
stealing oft his presentation.
He dispatched them to their heaven,
swift and sure the hatchet's blow.

How the Sharplet preened and boasted

When the Sharplet came to Loonhaunt,
to the shining great sea waters,
there he built a mighty image,
there to trick the noble fish-folk,
there to fool them into hunger.
He who knew not fish-folk thinking,
thought them simple, thought them dumb.

He affixed a cardboard image,
--nay, not graven, yet more grave--
he affixed a cardboard image,
nosegay, snot poop, vain defacement,
made of cardboard, made of wire,
told the fish-folk he knew better,
knew far better them to please.

Yet returned he, vanquished, downcast,
in the evening, showing naught.
Wendy laughed from 'mongst the trees,
saw his folly from the trees,
saw him walk the dock, no booty.
Nary minnow brought he home.

How the Loonhaunt fish scorned Sharplet!
Snickered fulsome 'neath the waves!
How the Loonhaunt fish praised Swanee,
He who knew the skill of plastics,
He who learned at foot of Harber,
Mighty Harber, priest to UMCO.

How Sharplet sought some status

Hear how Sharplet bought fine raiment,
that the five serve UMCO better.
Hear how Sharplet 'plied for priesthood,
Wore the raiment, spoke of lore.

Yet he came not to the priesthood,
came not Sharplet to the priesthood,
though he sought it year on year.
Sharplet knew not of proceedings,
chaired by Harber, viewed by Swanee,
in the boardrooms of the UMCO,
in the august halls of state,
where twice yearly there are motions,
votings, plannings, all to 'vance the UMCO's weal.

> These are tales of daily fishing,
> tales of men who know the Northland,
> tales of men who go out boldly,
> cherish boxes made in commerce,
> cherish boxes made by UMCO.
> These are men who honor UMCO,
> priesthood of the mighty Harber,
> he who brought the men to waters,
> to the shining great sea waters,
> to the Kish-ku-tee-nah mighty,
> to the Loonhaunt home of winds.

How the Swanee made his cornpone

As the Swanee made his corn pone,
working 'longside faithful Swanling
--he who found the brock-oh-lee-ah,
he who made it noble, different,
he who served it o'er and o'er--

Swanee cleaned the skillet grimy,
Swanee using many towels,
towels of paper, Minn-ah-so-tan,
They for cleaning being best.

As the Swanee made his cornpone,
Saw he proudly how the Swanling
conjured, blended, found new flavors,
called on Sharplet for his aid.

Swanling wasted not a morsel,
made good use of every purchase,
wasted not the toonies' value,
wasted not the loonies' shine.

He who stocked the larder fulsome,
stood by Swanee making corn pone,
cleaning skillet, tiring not.
Swanee closed his ears to censure,
closed his ears to crit-ee-sizz-um,
words which spoke of "far too crispy,"
"far too hard to chew this stuff."
These were words well known to Swanee,
having heard them oft before.

Swanee learned this skill from Swann One,
not from Swann Two, noble father.
Learned he cornpone from the sourceman,
only water, salt, and meal.
At the knee of his grandfather
learned he cornpone for his friends.
At the knee of his grandfather,
At the knee of Swanee One,
Did he copy, question, follow.

Swanee Two did not make corn pone.
This did fall to Swanee Three,
fell to Swanee, here with brother,
with the noble larder-stocker,
he who found the brock-oh-lee-ah,
he who wasted not a morsel,
he who kept the reckonings tidy,
he who knew how many loonies,
many toonies, many dollars
needed he to stock his larder.

How the Harber froze his digits

There they worked, the Swanee brothers,
aided oft by Sharplet eager
(he who built the loathsome image),
aided oft by Apple Chopper
(he who swings the winsome rod,
he who killed the baby pikelets).
Harber labored in the fish house,
daily labored, failing not,
skinning Loonhaunt's mighty creatures,
using tools which Swanfly honed.

He who daily skinned the creatures,
cut the creatures, boned and skinned them,
he who froze full off his digits,
doing duty in the fish house,
thinking only of his duty
(yet occasionally of libation),
he who daily earned libation,
cleaning creatures in the fish house,
he who suffered freezing fingers,
whilst the Swanee worked in warmth.

Yet the Harber labored onward,
labored suffering in the coolth,
while the Swanfly chopped the apples,
while the Sharplet tended fire,
while the foursome worked in warmness,
labored Harber in the coolth.

There he labored in the fish house,
in the fish house with no heating,
where he daily froze his fingers.
Yet he went there, went there daily,
fearing lest he have to cook.

Yet, he did cook--rare occasion!--
when the Swanfly gave him apples,
when the Swanfly did that bidding.
Then he made the mighty skillet,
filled with apples, filled with sugar,
even sin-ah-mon went in there,
butter, sugar, even salt.

On the shore of shining waters,
salt he added to the apples,
to the apples chopped by Swanfly,
to the apples peeled by Swanfly.
He, the Swanfly, ne'er complaining,
laboring onward, sous-chef faithful,
laboring steadfast, for the Harber.

How the Swanee furnished fatwood

Hear how Swanee purchased fatwood
From online, from Am-a-zonah,
From the mines of Cyberspace-ah.
Hear how fatwood brought the fine flames,
Aided by the bark of birches,
Aided by much greasy paper.

Some inveighed against the fatwood--
Nay, not "some," 'twas only Harber--
Called it "foolish waste of money."
Yet the Swanee bought the fatwood,
Tricked the Harber, priest of UMCO,
Hid it in his gear and tackle.
Harber shipped it it U-P-S-ah.
Saved the Sharplet many grumblings,
Saved the Swanling, prone to cursing,
Dark invectives laced with "f" words.

Should you ask me, whence these stories?
Whence these legends and traditions?
Whence the odors of the forest
with the dew and damp of meadows,
with the curling smoke of pinewood,
split by Sharplet, daily done?
I should answer, I should tell you,
"From the forests and the prairies,
from the great lakes of the Northland,
from the land of Kish-ku-tee-nah,
from the land of Loonhaunt mighty,
from that land our northern home."

25th Anniversary

In the blink of an eye the years went by,
The years with you,
My blink-of-an-eye darling.
Each year glorious?
No, definitely not.
There was tough stuff.
But you were there.
That made all the difference.
You were there, God love you.
Always there. Always ready:
With a Band-Aid (hard to open);
With a fast trip to UT hospital;
Or to wherever I was.
God love you,
You were there.
That made all the difference.
You were there.

Croakers and court

KIRKSEY'S DAUGHTER HAD STOOD AT THE PIER RAIL FOR HOURS, throwing out the weighted line, catching croakers and laughing, pulling them up the thirty feet of air, calling out, "I've got a big one, Daddy!" knowing it wasn't true, just happy to be catching fish. She'd hold the fish and carefully back the hook out, throw him back: "Bye, bye, Mr. Croaker. Go tell your big brother to bite my hook."

He'd taught her to put squid on the line. She would bait up and throw the line out again, the white strips waving in the air, flying from the top-and-bottom rig, two ounces of pyramidal lead pulling them down, taking the rig hard into the rolling waves and to the bottom. Twenty-pound mono, Kirksey knew it was overkill for these little fish, but then you might catch a ray or even a shark, and then what would you do, if you had six-pound test?

In thirty seconds she'd have another. She had learned to reel back in just until the line was gently taut, that was tricky, and wait hardly breathing for the tug. It took a while for her to learn to keep the line just so, not bounce the weight across the bottom. Until she got the feel for it she would think she had a fish, feeling the pull of the bouncing lead, while the fish stripped off the squid.

It was a lot like raising children, Kirksey thought. You couldn't be slack or you'd miss the clues. And you couldn't tight-line them either, not kids, or you'd bounce them, get false signals, think you'd found things that needed fixing, try to fix them, get no fish, wonder why.

Kirksey had heard the litany of failures over and over in court. The tales of parenting gone bad, glaring incidents, small failures. His docket was now mostly domestic, a welcome change from search and seizure, endless motions, suppression hearings. It's not the issues which were better in domestic court, nothing could beat the criminal law for intellectual content, it was that in family law there was the chance that he could help. He knew he did help, sorting out others' problems well enough to give their kids a chance to climb.

So, sitting in a black robe, he the putative swift and sure dispenser of perfect solutions, he knew he only had a chance at being useful if he listened carefully to the parents' words, listened carefully to the children's stumbling, embarrassed, often coached mumblings. Kirksey had a chance if he thought hard about what was really going on, if he listened for successes in school, in sports, in music lessons, and from all that maybe built a trellis for the vines to climb.

Schizophrenia and certainty

I AM HEAVILY VESTED IN MY OWN VERSION OF REALITY. "MY WAY OF analyzing things is the only correct way. That's obvious, right? So here's the deal. Here is what we are going to do."

My father was a great diagnostician. Perhaps one needs cocksure confidence to pronounce diagnoses. When I was a judge, I had such firm confidence in my legal abilities that I "knew" how a case should be understood and then dealt with. But my twelve law clerks taught me, one after another, that there were other ways than mine to understand a case. I learned that there were creative, different, ways of thinking about the same grist.

Getting to know Mr. X has been mind-changing for me. He had schizophrenia and was "incurable." When I heard of his delusions, I knew he was crazy. End of discussion.

But then, I read his 2008 write-up done by Bertram P. Karon, a psychology professor at Michigan State. The "reality" of Mr. X, was his own valid reality. I learned that it deserved attention, validation, and then, perhaps, some help to guide him back to "our" common, shared Aristotelian reality where a table is a table, an umbrella is an umbrella. Where the umbrella isn't proof that people are out to get Mr. X.

There is a parallel between the usual psychiatric handling of schizophrenics and what lawyers do in the criminal justice system. Both arenas want their stressors to go away. In psychiatry that means meds and/or electrotherapy--or in the time of Mr. X it meant that. That he has been improperly handled is not even recognized.

A lesser example of this occurs in medicine generally: The patient wants relief, the doctor wants to move on, the patient feels happier if given a drug, any drug, something to walk out with. So the doctor prescribes the drug simply to get rid of the patient.

In the law, the press of the criminal justice docket produces motivation for district attorneys to offer plea compromises. At the outset, the defendant has been multiply charged, often overcharged. "Throw the book at him." Then in the negotiation phase, it is suggested that some of the counts will be voluntarily withdrawn, if the defendant will plead to something lesser. The defendant wants his freedom, he has been unable to make bond--or, if able to make bond, he still wants to dispose of the pending charges. So the defendant pleads to something lesser, and gets convicted of the lesser count(s). He has freedom, or a reduced incarceration.

But take the case of the defendant innocent of everything. He has been wrongly arrested. He faces multiple counts, and is urged to accept a lesser plea. He is innocent. He knows it. The likelihood is that he will plead. His attorney does not want him to go to trial. The prosecutor does not want to try the case. The defendant's family wants him back, not risking all on the dice-roll of a trial. So he pleads. In a fair world he would not have been presented with the dilemma.

The White Rose

THE **WHITE ROSE** (DIE *WEISSE ROSE*) WAS A NON-VIOLENT, intellectual resistance group in Nazi Germany led by students from the University of Munich. The group conducted an anonymous leaflet and graffiti campaign that called for active opposition to the Nazi regime.

Their activities started in Munich 27 June 1942. The activities ended with the arrest of the core group by the Gestapo 18 February 1943. Hans and Sophie Scholl were handing out flyers at the Ludwig Maximilian University of Munich when they were caught by the custodian, Jakob Schmid, who informed the Gestapo. They, as well as other members and supporters of the group who carried on distributing the pamphlets, faced show trials by the Nazi People's Court (*Volksgerichtshof*), and many of them were sentenced to death or imprisonment.

Hans and Sophie Scholl and Christoph Probst were executed by guillotine four days after their arrest. During the trial, Sophie interrupted the judge multiple times. No defendants were given any opportunity to speak.

The group wrote, printed, and initially distributed their pamphlets in the greater Munich region. Later, secret carriers brought copies to other cities, mostly in the southern parts of Germany. In total, the White Rose authored six leaflets, which were multiplied and spread, about 15,000 copies. In their second leaflet, they denounced the persecution and mass murder of the Jews.

22 February 1943 they were sentenced to death by the People's Court, led by Judge-President Roland Freisler. They were executed by guillotine the same day in the Stadelheim Prison. Their grave is in the adjacent Perlacher Forst cemetery (grave number 73-1-18/19).

Ants and matches

WHEN KIRKSEY WAS A CHILD AT HIS GRANDFATHER'S HOUSE IN GEORGIA, his grandfather would pay him a penny for each black ant Kirksey killed. So for his entire time in Georgia the boy stepped on ants, all around the yard, counting up his wealth. On one day he made sixty-eight cents.

His grandfather let him have matches, too, the ones from behind the kitchen door, all he wanted, and Kirksey would light matches in the yard, on the side of the sandbox, on the shed door, not really possible on tree bark, good on rocks if they were big enough and flat enough, OK on the side of the house, or underneath the house on the brick pilings that held up the floor joists, and under there you could use the stub of a candle to burn cobwebs from between the stringers, rusty nails poking down at you through the flooring, the people walking around upstairs, the floor boards bowing a little and sighing, Kirksey hearing words but not understanding them, like the people were underwater or far away in a dream, and best of all, they didn't know Kirksey was there.

Bears and hummingbirds

LAST YEAR KIRKSEY HAD GOTTEN TO KNOW A MOTHER BEAR AND HER four cubs. They became his friends, as much as it was possible for a human being to be friendly with bears. But he was always glad to see them. The cubs would wrestle, tumbling on the deck between the chairs. They would climb on the railing and walk. They would eat dogwood berries from the trees they could reach from the banister. Kirksey's deck was a playground.

When the second year arrived, the cubs came back. At least he thought these new bears were the cubs. The mother bear did not come back. The bears were interested in the hummingbird feeder. They would look at it, but they could not reach it. As the summer continued, the bears got taller and taller and were almost but not quite able to reach the feeder and pull it down.

In October no hummingbirds had been to the feeder for days, so Kirksey believed they had all migrated. His brother in upper New York state thought so too. So Kirksey took the hummingbird feeder down. The bears continued to come. They looked for the hummingbird feeder.

Earlier, Kirksey had had seed feeders for the birds. They had hung down from the eaves of the cabin far enough that a grown bear could easily reach them. When Kirksey saw he was about to lose a feeder, he would shoot the bear with his .22 pistol loaded with number 12 shot. The shot was tiny, almost dust. It did not hurt the bear, but it did alarm him. A loud noise and lots of smoke. Kirksey was careful not to shoot the bear in his face. But eventually the bears destroyed each of the seed feeders. So Kirksey stopped buying them.

Butterball

KIRKSEY HAD READ THAT THERE HAD BEEN A DISCUSSION AMONG THE
Founding Fathers as to whether the wild turkey or the eagle should be
the national bird. They knew the bird chosen would become our totem,
our sacred object. It would be an emblem for all Americans. Benjamin
Franklin had plumped for the turkey and he had lost, so the bald eagle
became America's national bird, and Franklin had had to go to Paris to
chase women, or peace, or something.

Still, Kirksey thought, if the turkey had won, there might have been
coins with the turkey. At first it would certainly have been the tall
angular wild version: bearded, wily, intelligent, friend of the Pilgrims.
But with the passage of time, and the changing of the turkey itself, the
coins would feature today's turkey, the Butterball. It would fit snugly
on the back of a coin, a half dollar say, all trussed up and frozen, plastic
protective wrap gleaming under fishnet, drumsticks poking up against
the plastic, ankle bones straining to be released into the American oven.

For this coin there would be no scrabbly horned feet to render through
meticulous engraving, no delicate overlapping of primary and secondary
feathers, no flaring tail in strut or trailing in flight. It would be the
Butterball as we know him in the freezer case. There could even be a
larger coin, the silver dollar perhaps, with the family gathered round
to eat the totem. Butterball atop the family table, roasted and aromatic,
wisps of steam suggested by the engraver.

How different would America's politics be, her resolve and national
purpose, if several times a year, Christmas and Thanksgiving at least,
America ate the totem? It would set her apart from feckless nations, the
French for example, who have no totem at all, or the Canadians, who
have a totem they cannot eat, the state of Florida.

The Butterball of today, after a few short generations of inbreeding, has become luscious and heavy-breasted, with delicate and thoughtful segregations of white and dark meat.

Ben Franklin had simply been wrong for once in his life. The man who had flown the kite and invented eyeglasses had had to go to France, defeated, to live for years with people of no totem and very few consonants.

Clean socks

KIRKSEY LOVED CLEAN SOCKS, ESPECIALLY THE RAGG SOCKS HIS BAILIFF had given him for Christmas, thick warm and comfortable socks. Kirksey thought he might be turning into a boring guy, someone with no zip, but there it was: He loved taking a pair of clean ragg socks out of his suitcase when he was on a trip, say, and smell the smell of home, unroll and stretch the socks, and pull them on. What a bore.

Or was it just clean joy in simple things? The stuff Julie Andrews sang about,

> *Raindrops on roses and whiskers on kittens*
> *Bright copper kettles and warm woollen mittens*
> *Brown paper packages tied up with strings*
> *These are a few of my favorite things*

Maybe so, maybe it was clean joy, maybe all was well, maybe socks were just part of his personal list of favorite things.

Football

In high school Kirksey had played football against TSD, the Tennessee School for the Deaf. A strong team. And dirty too. Kirksey could not remember whether Webb had won or lost. He did remember that Webb had posted a four-out-of-seven season. Since that was the first year Webb had had a football team, that was pretty good.

TSD snapped the ball whenever they were ready. Kirksey didn't know how they knew when they were ready. There was no calling signals. TSD also pinched you in the pile ups. That was new.

Kirksey had played both ways, offense and defense. He had been in the line because his eyesight was bad without glasses. He could have been in the backfield as a runner, but coach had better ball carriers than Kirksey. Shuttleworth was really good, and he could catch passes. He could see them coming.

In high school Kirksey had sold Cokes at UT football games. On a good day Kirksey would make seven dollars. He carried rectangular buckets filled with ice up and down the aisles. Cokes and also 7 Ups in glass bottles. Kirksey would pull the cap off with a flourish and make it fly away. Then he would pour the drink into a cup and pass the cup down the row to the customer, who would pass money back. Drinks cost twenty cents. Often Kirksey would be paid with a quarter which was very very good. There was some finesse in serving 7 Ups, because sometimes there would be dirt in the cup. So Kirksey would save that cup and use it for Cokes.

He had been at the 1958 UT-Chattanooga game when Chattanooga defeated Tennessee. This was unheard of. Chattanooga fans stormed the field and tore down the goal posts. Police intervened massively, which prolonged what became a riot. It lasted for hours, on the field and later on Cumberland Avenue. Kirksey thought the whole thing was marvellous, he having never seen a riot before.

Kentucky games were always cold, being at the end of the season. Often there was snow. At one of them, Kirksey had thrown snowballs from his seat in Section S, Row 30 at the backs of the Kentucky players.

On November 25, 1950, Kentucky lost to Tennessee 0-7. It was the team's only loss that year. Kentucky was coached by Bear Bryant, and it was the number one team in the nation.

Hungary and Latin

AFTER COLLEGE, KIRKSEY SPENT A YEAR IN AUSTRIA STUDYING GERMAN literature to get ready for graduate school. His German became so good he could pass for a native of Styria, Austria's Steiermark. In the spring of 1965, he took a short bus ride to Budapest.

After three hours in Budapest, he was disoriented, unhappy. The landscape was not different from Austria, and Budapest was a big city like Vienna. Kirksey walked the streets feeling worse and worse. He went from one place to another, using his guidebook. He took some pictures from the hill, drank a glass of tea. Even the tea failed to lift his mood.

At the summit of the hill was St. Stephen's cathedral. The guidebook said he should go. Kirksey didn't care. He felt rootless, lost. He wanted to check out of his hotel, walk to the bus station, and get back to Austria. What was it about Hungary? Was he getting sick? He hadn't eaten anything strange, none of those sausages with names he didn't recognize. He had eaten a roll, played it safe. Kirksey felt lost inside an Ingmar Bergman film without words.

He pushed his way into the cathedral, dropped a few coins in the collection box, and gazed at the stained glass windows. He felt better at once. There were words there he could read. Latin, wonderful Latin. It was in the windows, on the grave markers, at the stations of the cross. Kirksey felt his miasma lift. He could read again. He had the written word back, the Western tradition, he knew where he was. No more impossible Ugric lump words, not a cognate anywhere, the simplest everyday vocabulary beyond his grasp. He loved this church, its architecture. He liked Hungary fine. He was glad he had come.

Hansel and Gretel

I HAVE WRITTEN ABOUT THE BROTHERS GRIMM BEFORE: IN MY 2021 *Kirksey* ("How the Children Played Butchering with Each Other"). To understate the situation, the Grimms did not sanitize what they collected from the German landscape of oral tradition, no matter how horrible the content. Disney of course did, and you can be of two minds about that. All in all, it is probably better to wait for adulthood before learning the truth about Cinderella, about Snow White, and about Hansel and Gretel's wicked stepmother and their devoted but feckless father.

Judge for yourself:

Hänsel und Gretel	Hansel and Gretel
Vor einem großen Walde wohnte ein armer Holzhacker mit seiner Frau und seinen zwei Kindern; das Bübchen hieß Hänsel und das Mädchen Gretel. Er hatte wenig zu beißen und zu brechen, und einmal, als große Teuerung ins Land kam, konnte er das tägliche Brot nicht mehr schaffen.	Near by a great forest dwelt a poor wood-cutter with his wife and his two children. The boy was called Hansel and the girl Gretel. He had little to bite and to break, and once when great famine fell on the land, he could no longer procure even daily bread.
Wie er sich nun abends im Bette Gedanken machte und sich vor Sorgen herumwälzte, seufzte er und sprach zu seiner Frau: "Was soll aus uns werden? Wie können wir unsere armen Kinder ernähren da wir für uns selbst nichts mehr haben?" -	Now when he thought this over by night in his bed, and tossed about in his anxiety, he groaned and said to his wife: 'What is to become of us? How are we to feed our poor children, when we no longer have anything even for ourselves?'

"Weißt du was, Mann," antwortete die Frau, "wir wollen morgen in aller Frühe die Kinder hinaus in den Wald führen, wo er am dicksten ist. Da machen wir ihnen ein Feuer an und geben jedem noch ein Stückchen Brot, dann gehen wir an unsere Arbeit und lassen sie allein. Sie finden den Weg nicht wieder nach Haus, und wir sind sie los." -

"Nein, Frau," sagte der Mann, "das tue ich nicht; wie sollt ich's übers Herz bringen, meine Kinder im Walde allein zu lassen! Die wilden Tiere würden bald kommen und sie zerreißen." - "Oh, du Narr," sagte sie, "dann müssen wir alle viere Hungers sterben, du kannst nur die Bretter für die Särge hobeln," und ließ ihm keine Ruhe, bis er einwilligte. "Aber die armen Kinder dauern mich doch," sagte der Mann.

Die zwei Kinder hatten vor Hunger auch nicht einschlafen können und hatten gehört, was die Stiefmutter zum Vater gesagt hatte. Gretel weinte bittere Tränen und sprach zu Hänsel: "Nun ist's um uns geschehen." -

"Still, Gretel," sprach Hänsel, "gräme dich nicht, ich will uns schon helfen." Und als die Alten eingeschlafen waren, stand er auf, zog sein Röcklein an, machte die Untertüre auf und schlich sich hinaus. Da schien der Mond ganz hell, und die weißen Kieselsteine, die vor dem Haus lagen, glänzten wie lauter Batzen. Hänsel bückte sich und steckte so viele in sein Rocktäschlein, als nur hinein wollten. Dann ging er wieder zurück, sprach zu Gretel: "Sei getrost, liebes Schwesterchen, und schlaf nur ruhig ein, Gott wird uns nicht verlassen," und legte sich wieder in sein Bett.

'I'll tell you what, husband,' answered the woman, 'early tomorrow morning we will take the children out into the forest to where it is the thickest; there we will light a fire for them, and give each of them one more piece of bread, and then we will go to our work and leave them alone. They will not find the way home again, and we shall be rid of them.'

'No, wife,' said the man, 'I will not do that; how can I bear to leave my children alone in the forest?—the wild animals would soon come and tear them to pieces.' 'O, you fool!' said she, 'then we must all four die of hunger, you may as well plane the planks for our coffins,' and she left him no peace until he consented. 'But I feel very sorry for the poor children, all the same,' said the man.

The two children had also not been able to sleep because of hunger, and had heard what their stepmother had said to their father. Gretel wept bitter tears, and said to Hansel: 'Now all is over with us.'

'Be quiet, Gretel,' said Hansel, 'do not distress yourself, I will soon find a way to help us.' And when the old folks had fallen asleep, he got up, put on his little coat, opened the door below, and crept outside. The moon shone brightly, and the white pebbles which lay in front of the house glittered like real silver pennies. Hansel stooped and stuffed the little pocket of his coat with as many as he could get in. Then he went back and said to Gretel: 'Be comforted, dear little sister, and sleep in peace, God will not forsake us,' and he lay down again in his bed.

Als der Tag anbrach, noch ehe die Sonne aufgegangen war, kam schon die Frau und weckte die beiden Kinder: "Steht auf, ihr Faulenzer, wir wollen in den Wald gehen und Holz holen."

When day dawned, but before the sun had risen, the woman came and awoke the two children, saying: 'Get up, you sluggards! we are going into the forest to fetch wood.'

Dann gab sie jedem ein Stückchen Brot und sprach: "Da habt ihr etwas für den Mittag, aber eßt's nicht vorher auf, weiter kriegt ihr nichts." Gretel nahm das Brot unter die Schürze, weil Hänsel die Steine in der Tasche hatte. Danach machten sie sich alle zusammen auf den Weg nach dem Wald.

She gave each a little piece of bread, and said: 'There is something for your dinner, but do not eat it up before then, for you will get nothing else.' Gretel took the bread under her apron, as Hansel had the pebbles in his pocket. Then they all set out together on the way to the forest.

Als sie ein Weilchen gegangen waren, stand Hänsel still und guckte nach dem Haus zurück und tat das wieder und immer wieder. Der Vater sprach: "Hänsel, was guckst du da und bleibst zurück, hab acht und vergiß deine Beine nicht!" -

When they had walked a short time, Hansel stood still and peeped back at the house, and did so again and again. His father said: 'Hansel, what are you looking at there and staying behind for? Pay attention, and do not forget how to use your legs.'

"Ach, Vater," sagte Hänsel, "ich sehe nach meinem weißen Kätzchen, das sitzt oben auf dem Dach und will mir Ade sagen."

'Ah, father,' said Hansel, 'I am looking at my little white cat, which is sitting up on the roof, and wants to say goodbye to me.'

Die Frau sprach: "Narr, das ist dein Kätzchen nicht, das ist die Morgensonne, die auf den Schornstein scheint." Hänsel aber hatte nicht nach dem Kätzchen gesehen, sondern immer einen von den blanken Kieselsteinen aus seiner Tasche auf den Weg geworfen.

The wife said: 'Fool, that is not your little cat, that is the morning sun which is shining on the chimneys.' Hansel, however, had not been looking back at the cat, but had been constantly throwing one of the white pebble-stones out of his pocket on the road.

Als sie mitten in den Wald gekommen waren, sprach der Vater: "Nun sammelt Holz, ihr Kinder, ich will ein Feuer anmachen, damit ihr nicht friert." Hänsel und Gretel trugen Reisig zusammen, einen kleinen Berg hoch. Das Reisig ward angezündet, und als die Flamme recht hoch brannte, sagte die Frau:

"Nun legt euch ans Feuer, ihr Kinder, und ruht euch aus, wir gehen in den Wald und hauen Holz. Wenn wir fertig sind, kommen wir wieder und holen euch ab."

Hänsel und Gretel saßen um das Feuer, und als der Mittag kam, aß jedes sein Stücklein Brot. Und weil sie die Schläge der Holzaxt hörten, so glaubten sie, ihr Vater wär' in der Nähe. Es war aber nicht die Holzaxt, es war ein Ast, den er an einen dürren Baum gebunden hatte und den der Wind hin und her schlug.

Und als sie so lange gesessen hatten, fielen ihnen die Augen vor Müdigkeit zu, und sie schliefen fest ein. Als sie endlich erwachten, war es schon finstere Nacht. Gretel fing an zu weinen und sprach: "Wie sollen wir nun aus dem Wald kommen?" Hänsel aber tröstete sie: "Wart nur ein Weilchen, bis der Mond aufgegangen ist, dann wollen wir den Weg schon finden." Und als der volle Mond aufgestiegen war, so nahm Hänsel sein Schwesterchern an der Hand und ging den Kieselsteinen nach, die schimmerten wie neugeschlagene Batzen und zeigten ihnen den Weg.

When they had reached the middle of the forest, the father said: 'Now, children, pile up some wood, and I will light a fire so that you may not be cold.' Hansel and Gretel gathered brushwood together, as high as a little hill. The brushwood was lit, and when the flames were burning very high, the woman said:

'Now, children, lay yourselves down by the fire and rest, we will go into the forest and cut some wood. When we are done, we will come back and fetch you away.'

Hansel and Gretel sat by the fire, and when noon came, each ate a little piece of bread, and as they heard the strokes of the wood-axe they believed that their father was near. It was not the axe, however, but a branch which he had fastened to a withered tree which the wind was blowing backwards and forwards.

And as they had been sitting for such a long time, their eyes closed with fatigue, and they fell fast asleep. When at last they awoke, it was already dark night. Gretel began to cry and said: 'How are we to get out of the forest now?' But Hansel comforted her and said: 'Just wait a little, until the moon has risen, and then we will soon find the way.'

And when the full moon had risen, Hansel took his little sister by the hand, and followed the pebbles which shone like newly-coined silver pieces, and showed them the way.

Sie gingen die ganze Nacht hindurch und kamen bei anbrechendem Tag wieder zu ihres Vaters Haus. Sie klopften an die Tür, und als die Frau aufmachte und sah, daß es Hänsel und Gretel waren, sprach sie:

They walked the whole night long, and by break of day came once more to their father's house. They knocked at the door, and when the woman opened it and saw that it was Hansel and Gretel, she said:

"Ihr bösen Kinder, was habt ihr so lange im Walde geschlafen, wir haben geglaubt, ihr wollet gar nicht wiederkommen." Der Vater aber freute sich, denn es war ihm zu Herzen gegangen, daß er sie so allein zurückgelassen hatte.

'You naughty children, why have you slept so long in the forest?—we thought you were never coming back at all!' The father, however, rejoiced, for it had cut him to the heart to leave them behind alone.

Nicht lange danach war wieder Not in allen Ecken, und die Kinder hörten, wie die Mutter nachts im Bette zu dem Vater sprach: "Alles ist wieder aufgezehrt, wir haben noch einen halben Laib Brot, hernach hat das Lied ein Ende. Die Kinder müssen fort, wir wollen sie tiefer in den Wald hineinführen, damit sie den Weg nicht wieder herausfinden; es ist sonst keine Rettung für uns."

Not long afterwards, there was once more great dearth throughout the land, and the children heard their mother saying at night to their father: 'Everything is eaten again, we have one half loaf left, and that is the end. The children must go, we will take them farther into the woods, so that they will not find their way out again; there is no other means of saving ourselves!'

Dem Mann fiel's schwer aufs Herz, und er dachte: Es wäre besser, daß du den letzten Bissen mit deinen Kindern teiltest. Aber die Frau hörte auf nichts, was er sagte, schalt ihn und machte ihm Vorwürfe.

The man's heart was heavy, and he thought: 'It would be better for you to share the last mouthful with your children.' The woman, however, would listen to nothing that he had to say, but scolded and reproached him.

Wer A sagt, muß B sagen, und weil er das erstemal nachgegeben hatte, so mußte er es auch zum zweitenmal.

He who says A must say B, likewise, and as he had yielded the first time, he had to do so a second time also.

Die Kinder waren aber noch wach gewesen und hatten das Gespräch mitangehört. Als die Alten schliefen, stand Hänsel wieder auf, wollte hinaus und die Kieselsteine auflesen, wie das vorigemal; aber die Frau hatte die Tür verschlossen, und Hänsel konnte nicht heraus. Aber er tröstete sein Schwesterchen und sprach: "Weine nicht, Gretel, und schlaf nur ruhig, der liebe Gott wird uns schon helfen."

The children, however, were still awake and had heard the conversation. When the old folks were asleep, Hansel again got up, and wanted to go out and pick up pebbles as he had done before, but the woman had locked the door, and Hansel could not get out. Nevertheless he comforted his little sister, and said: 'Do not cry, Gretel, go to sleep quietly, the good God will help us.'

Am frühen Morgen kam die Frau und holte die Kinder aus dem Bette. Sie erhielten ihr Stückchen Brot, das war aber noch kleiner als das vorigemal. Auf dem Wege nach dem Wald bröckelte es Hänsel in der Tasche, stand oft still und warf ein Bröcklein auf die Erde.

Early in the morning came the woman, and took the children out of their beds. Their piece of bread was given to them, but it was still smaller than the time before. On the way into the forest Hansel crumbled his in his pocket, and often stood still and threw a morsel on the ground.

"Hänsel, was stehst du und guckst dich um?" sagte der Vater, "geh deiner Wege!" - "Ich sehe nach meinem Täubchen, das sitzt auf dem Dache und will mir Ade sagen," antwortete Hänsel. "Narr," sagte die Frau, "das ist dein Täubchen nicht, das ist die Morgensonne, die auf den Schornstein oben scheint." Hänsel aber warf nach und nach alle Bröcklein auf den Weg.

'Hansel, why do you stop and look round?' said the father, 'go on.' 'I am looking back at my little pigeon which is sitting on the roof, and wants to say goodbye to me,' answered Hansel. 'Fool!' said the woman, 'that is not your little pigeon, that is the morning sun that is shining on the chimney.' Hansel, however little by little, threw all the crumbs on the path.

Die Frau führte die Kinder noch tiefer in den Wald, wo sie ihr Lebtag noch nicht gewesen waren. Da ward wieder ein großes Feuer angemacht, und die Mutter sagte:

The woman led the children still deeper into the forest, where they had never in their lives been before. Then a great fire was again made, and the mother said:

"Bleibt nur da sitzen, ihr Kinder, und wenn ihr müde seid, könnt ihr ein wenig schlafen. Wir gehen in den Wald und hauen Holz, und abends, wenn wir fertig sind, kommen wir und holen euch ab."

'Just sit there, you children, and when you are tired you may sleep a little; we are going into the forest to cut wood, and in the evening when we are done, we will come and fetch you away.'

Als es Mittag war, teilte Gretel ihr Brot mit Hänsel, der sein Stück auf den Weg gestreut hatte. Dann schliefen sie ein, und der Abend verging; aber niemand kam zu den armen Kindern. Sie erwachten erst in der finstern Nacht, und Hänsel tröstete sein Schwesterchen und sagte: "Wart nur, Gretel, bis der Mond aufgeht, dann werden wir die Brotbröcklein sehen, die ich ausgestreut habe, die zeigen uns den Weg nach Haus."
Als der Mond kam, machten sie sich auf, aber sie fanden kein Bröcklein mehr, denn die viel tausend Vögel, die im Walde und im Felde umherfliegen, die hatten sie weggepickt.

Hänsel sagte zu Gretel: "Wir werden den Weg schon finden." Aber sie fanden ihn nicht. Sie gingen die ganze Nacht und noch einen Tag von Morgen bis Abend, aber sie kamen aus dem Wald nicht heraus und waren so hungrig, denn sie hatten nichts als die paar Beeren, die auf der Erde standen. Und weil sie so müde waren, daß die Beine sie nicht mehr tragen wollten, so legten sie sich unter einen Baum und schliefen ein.

Nun war's schon der dritte Morgen, daß sie ihres Vaters Haus verlassen hatten. Sie fingen wieder an zu gehen, aber sie gerieten immer tiefer in den Wald, und wenn nicht bald Hilfe kam, mußten sie verschmachten.

When it was noon, Gretel shared her piece of bread with Hansel, who had scattered his by the way. Then they fell asleep and evening passed, but no one came to the poor children. They did not awake until it was dark, and Hansel comforted his little sister and said: 'Just wait, Gretel, until the moon rises, and then we shall see the crumbs of bread which I have strewn about, they will show us our way home again.'
When the moon came they set out, but they found no crumbs, for the many thousands of birds which fly about in the woods and fields had pecked them all up.

Hansel said to Gretel: 'We shall soon find the way,' but they did not find it. They walked the whole night and all the next day too from morning till evening, but they did not get out of the forest, and were very hungry, for they had nothing to eat but two or three berries, which grew on the ground. And as they were so weary that their legs would carry them no longer, they lay down beneath a tree and fell asleep.

It was now three mornings since they had left their father's house. They began to walk again, but they always came deeper into the forest, and if help did not come soon, they would die of hunger and weariness.

Als es Mittag war, sahen sie ein schönes, schneeweißes Vögelein auf einem Ast sitzen, das sang so schön, daß sie stehen blieben und ihm zuhörten. Und als es fertig war, schwang es seine Flügel und flog vor ihnen her, und sie gingen ihm nach, bis sie zu einem Häuschen gelangten, auf dessen Dach es sich setzte, und als sie ganz nahe herankamen, so sahen sie, daß das Häuslein aus Brot gebaut war und mit Kuchen gedeckt; aber die Fenster waren von hellem Zucker.

"Da wollen wir uns dranmachen," sprach Hänsel, "und eine gesegnete Mahlzeit halten. Ich will ein Stück vom Dach essen, Gretel, du kannst vom Fenster essen, das schmeckt süß." Hänsel reichte in die Höhe und brach sich ein wenig vom Dach ab, um zu versuchen, wie es schmeckte, und Gretel stellte sich an die Scheiben und knupperte daran.

Da rief eine feine Stimme aus der Stube heraus: "Knupper, knupper, Kneischen, Wer knuppert an meinem Häuschen?"

Die Kinder antworteten: "Der Wind, der Wind, Das himmlische Kind," und aßen weiter, ohne sich irre machen zu lassen. Hänsel, dem das Dach sehr gut schmeckte, riß sich ein großes Stück davon herunter, und Gretel stieß eine ganze runde Fensterscheibe heraus, setzte sich nieder und tat sich wohl damit. Da ging auf einmal die Türe auf, und eine steinalte Frau, die sich auf eine Krücke stützte, kam herausgeschlichen.

When it was mid-day, they saw a beautiful snow-white bird sitting on a bough, which sang so delightfully that they stood still and listened to it. And when its song was over, it spread its wings and flew away before them, and they followed it until they reached a little house, on the roof of which it alighted; and when they approached the little house they saw that it was built of bread and covered with cakes, but that the windows were of clear sugar.

'We will set to work on that,' said Hansel, 'and have a good meal. I will eat a bit of the roof, and you Gretel, can eat some of the window, it will taste sweet.' Hansel reached up above, and broke off a little of the roof to try how it tasted, and Gretel leant against the window and nibbled at the panes.

Then a soft voice cried from the parlour: 'Nibble, nibble, gnaw, Who is nibbling at my little house?'

The children answered: 'The wind, the wind, The heaven-born wind,' and went on eating without disturbing themselves. Hansel, who liked the taste of the roof, tore down a great piece of it, and Gretel pushed out the whole of one round window-pane, sat down, and enjoyed herself with it. Suddenly the door opened, and a woman as old as the hills, who supported herself on crutches, came creeping out.

Hänsel und Gretel erschraken so gewaltig, daß sie fallen ließen, was sie in den Händen hielten. Die Alte aber wackelte mit dem Kopfe und sprach: "Ei, ihr lieben Kinder, wer hat euch hierher gebracht? Kommt nur herein und bleibt bei mir, es geschieht euch kein Leid." Sie faßte beide an der Hand und führte sie in ihr Häuschen. Da ward ein gutes Essen aufgetragen, Milch und Pfannkuchen mit Zucker, Äpfel und Nüsse. Hernach wurden zwei schöne Bettlein weiß gedeckt, und Hänsel und Gretel legten sich hinein und meinten, sie wären im Himmel.

Die Alte hatte sich nur freundlich angestellt, sie war aber eine böse Hexe, die den Kindern auflauerte, und hatte das Brothäuslein bloß gebaut, um sie herbeizulocken. Wenn eins in ihre Gewalt kam, so machte sie es tot, kochte es und aß es, und das war ihr ein Festtag. Die Hexen haben rote Augen und können nicht weit sehen, aber sie haben eine feine Witterung wie die Tiere und merken's, wenn Menschen herankommen. Als Hänsel und Gretel in ihre Nähe kamen, da lachte sie boshaft und sprach höhnisch:

Hansel and Gretel were so terribly frightened that they let fall what they had in their hands. The old woman, however, nodded her head, and said: 'Oh, you dear children, who has brought you here? do come in, and stay with me. No harm shall happen to you.' She took them both by the hand, and led them into her little house. Then good food was set before them, milk and pancakes, with sugar, apples, and nuts. Afterwards two pretty little beds were covered with clean white linen, and Hansel and Gretel lay down in them, and thought they were in heaven.

The old woman had only pretended to be so kind; she was in reality a wicked witch, who lay in wait for children, and had only built the little house of bread in order to entice them there. When a child fell into her power, she killed it, cooked and ate it, and that was a feast day with her. Witches have red eyes, and cannot see far, but they have a keen scent like the beasts, and are aware when human beings draw near. When Hansel and Gretel came into her neighbourhood, she laughed with malice, and said mockingly:

"Die habe ich, die sollen mir nicht wieder entwischen!" Früh morgens, ehe die Kinder erwacht waren, stand sie schon auf, und als sie beide so lieblich ruhen sah, mit den vollen roten Backen, so murmelte sie vor sich hin: "Das wird ein guter Bissen werden."

Da packte sie Hänsel mit ihrer dürren Hand und trug ihn in einen kleinen Stall und sperrte ihn mit einer Gittertüre ein.

Er mochte schrein, wie er wollte, es half ihm nichts. Dann ging sie zur Gretel, rüttelte sie wach und rief:

"Steh auf, Faulenzerin, trag Wasser und koch deinem Bruder etwas Gutes, der sitzt draußen im Stall und soll fett werden.

Wenn er fett ist, so will ich ihn essen." Gretel fing an bitterlich zu weinen; aber es war alles vergeblich, sie mußte tun, was die böse Hexe verlangte.

Nun ward dem armen Hänsel das beste Essen gekocht, aber Gretel bekam nichts als Krebsschalen. Jeden Morgen schlich die Alte zu dem Ställchen und rief: "Hänsel, streck deine Finger heraus, damit ich fühle, ob du bald fett bist." Hänsel streckte ihr aber ein Knöchlein heraus, und die Alte, die trübe Augen hatte, konnte es nicht sehen und meinte, es wären Hänsels Finger, und verwunderte sich, daß er gar nicht fett werden wollte. Als vier Wochen herum waren und Hänsel immer mager blieb, da überkam sie die Ungeduld, und sie wollte nicht länger warten.

'I have them, they shall not escape me again!' Early in the morning before the children were awake, she was already up, and when she saw both of them sleeping and looking so pretty, with their plump and rosy cheeks she muttered to herself: 'That will be a dainty mouthful!' Then she seized Hansel with her shrivelled hand, carried him into a little stall, and locked him in behind a grated door.

Scream as he might, it would not help him. Then she went to Gretel, shook her till she awoke, and cried: 'Get up, lazy thing, fetch some water, and cook something good for your brother, he is in the stall outside, and is to be made fat.

When he is fat, I will eat him.' Gretel began to weep bitterly, but it was all in vain, for she was forced to do what the wicked witch commanded.

And now the best food was cooked for poor Hansel, but Gretel got nothing but crab-shells. Every morning the woman crept to the little stable, and cried: 'Hansel, stretch out your finger so that I may feel if you will soon be fat.' Hansel, however, stretched out a little bone to her, and the old woman, who had dim eyes, could not see it, and thought it was Hansel's finger, and was astonished that there was no way of fattening him. When four weeks had gone by, and Hansel still remained thin, she was seized with impatience and would not wait any longer.

"Heda, Gretel," rief sie dem Mädchen zu, "sei flink und trag Wasser! Hänsel mag fett oder mager sein, morgen will ich ihn schlachten und kochen."

Ach, wie jammerte das arme Schwesterchen, als es das Wasser tragen mußte, und wie flossen ihm die Tränen über die Backen herunter!

"Lieber Gott, hilf uns doch," rief sie aus, "hätten uns nur die wilden Tiere im Wald gefressen, so wären wir doch zusammen gestorben!" -

"Spar nur dein Geplärre," sagte die Alte, "es hilft dir alles nichts."

Frühmorgens mußte Gretel heraus, den Kessel mit Wasser aufhängen und Feuer anzünden.

"Erst wollen wir backen," sagte die Alte, "ich habe den Backofen schon eingeheizt und den Teig geknetet."

Sie stieß das arme Gretel hinaus zu dem Backofen, aus dem die Feuerflammen schon herausschlugen "Kriech hinein," sagte die Hexe, "und sieh zu, ob recht eingeheizt ist, damit wir das Brot hineinschieben können."

Und wenn Gretel darin war, wollte sie den Ofen zumachen und Gretel sollte darin braten, und dann wollte sie's aufessen. Aber Gretel merkte, was sie im Sinn hatte, und sprach:

"Ich weiß nicht, wie ich's machen soll; wie komm ich da hinein?" -

"Dumme Gans," sagte die Alte, "die Öffnung ist groß genug, siehst du wohl, ich könnte selbst hinein," krabbelte heran und steckte den Kopf in den Backofen.

Da gab ihr Gretel einen Stoß, daß sie weit hineinfuhr, machte die eiserne Tür zu und schob den Riegel vor.

Hu! Da fing sie an zu heulen, ganz grauselich; aber Gretel lief fort, und die böse Frau mußte elendiglich verbrennen.

'Now, then, Gretel,' she cried to the girl, 'stir yourself, and bring some water. Let Hansel be fat or lean, tomorrow I will kill him, and cook him.'

Ah, how the poor little sister did lament when she had to fetch the water, and how her tears did flow down her cheeks!

'Dear God, do help us,' she cried. 'If the wild beasts in the forest had but devoured us, we should at any rate have died together.'

'Just keep your noise to yourself,' said the old woman, 'it won't help you at all.'

Early in the morning, Gretel had to go out and hang up the cauldron with the water, and light the fire.

'We will bake first,' said the old woman, 'I have already heated the oven, and kneaded the dough.'

She pushed poor Gretel out to the oven, from which flames of fire were already darting. 'Creep in,' said the witch, 'and see if it is properly heated, so that we can put the bread in.'

And once Gretel was inside, she intended to shut the oven and let her bake in it, and then she would eat her, too. But Gretel saw what she had in mind, and said:

'I do not know how I am to do it; how do I get in?'

'Silly goose,' said the old woman. 'The door is big enough; just look, I can get in myself!' and she crept up and thrust her head into the oven.

Then Gretel gave her a push that drove her far into it, and shut the iron door, and fastened the bolt.

Oh! Then she began to howl quite terribly, but Gretel ran away and the evil woman was miserably burnt to death.

Gretel aber lief schnurstracks zum Hänsel, öffnete sein Ställchen und rief: "Hänsel, wir sind erlöst, die alte Hexe ist tot."

Gretel, however, ran like lightning to Hansel, opened his little stall, and cried: 'Hansel, we are saved! The old witch is dead!'

Da sprang Hänsel heraus wie ein Vogel aus dem Käfig, wenn ihm die Türe aufgemacht wird. Wie haben sie sich gefreut sind sich um den Hals gefallen, sind herumgesprungen und haben sich geküßt! Und weil sie sich nicht mehr zu fürchten brauchten, so gingen sie in das Haus der Hexe hinein. Da standen in allen Ecken Kasten mit Perlen und Edelsteinen. "Die sind noch besser als Kieselsteine," sagte Hänsel und steckte in seine Taschen, was hinein wollte. Und Gretel sagte:

Then Hansel sprang like a bird from its cage when the door is opened. How they did rejoice and embrace each other, and dance about and kiss each other! And as they had no longer any need to fear her, they went into the witch's house, and in every corner there stood chests full of pearls and jewels. 'These are far better than pebbles!' said Hansel, and thrust into his pockets whatever could be got in, and Gretel said:

"Ich will auch etwas mit nach Haus bringen," und füllte sein Schürzchen voll. "Aber jetzt wollen wir fort," sagte Hänsel, "damit wir aus dem Hexenwald herauskommen."

'I, too, will take something home with me,' and filled her pinafore full. 'But now we must be off,' said Hansel, 'that we may get out of the witch's forest.'

Als sie aber ein paar Stunden gegangen waren, gelangten sie an ein großes Wasser. "Wir können nicht hinüber," sprach Hänsel, "ich seh keinen Steg und keine Brücke." - "Hier fährt auch kein Schiffchen," antwortete Gretel, "aber da schwimmt eine weiße Ente, wenn ich die bitte, so hilft sie uns hinüber."

When they had walked for two hours, they came to a great stretch of water. 'We cannot cross,' said Hansel, 'I see no foot-plank, and no bridge.' 'And there is also no ferry,' answered Gretel, 'but a white duck is swimming there: if I ask her, she will help us over.'

Da rief sie: "Entchen, Entchen, Da steht Gretel und Hänsel. Kein Steg und keine Brücke, Nimm uns auf deinen weißen Rücken."

Then she cried: 'Little duck, little duck, dost thou see, Hansel and Gretel are waiting for thee? There's never a plank, or bridge in sight, Take us across on thy back so white.'

Das Entchen kam auch heran, und Hänsel setzte sich auf und bat sein Schwesterchen, sich zu ihm zu setzen. "Nein," antwortete Gretel, "es wird dem Entchen zu schwer, es soll uns nacheinander hinüberbringen."

Das tat das gute Tierchen, und als sie glücklich drüben waren und ein Weilchen fortgingen, da kam ihnen der Wald immer bekannter und immer bekannter vor, und endlich erblickten sie von weitem ihres Vaters Haus.

Da fingen sie an zu laufen, stürzten in die Stube hinein und fielen ihrem Vater um den Hals. Der Mann hatte keine frohe Stunde gehabt, seitdem er die Kinder im Walde gelassen hatte, die Frau aber war gestorben.

Gretel schüttelte sein Schürzchen aus, daß die Perlen und Edelsteine in der Stube herumsprangen, und Hänsel warf eine Handvoll nach der andern aus seiner Tasche dazu.

Da hatten alle Sorgen ein Ende, und sie lebten in lauter Freude zusammen.

Mein Märchen ist aus, dort lauft eine Maus, wer sie fängt, darf sich eine große Pelzkappe daraus machen.

The duck came to them, and Hansel seated himself on its back, and told his sister to sit by him. 'No,' replied Gretel, 'that will be too heavy for the little duck; she shall take us across, one after the other.'

The good little duck did so, and when they were once safely across and had walked for a short time, the forest seemed to be more and more familiar to them, and at length they saw from afar their father's house.

Then they began to run, rushed into the parlour, and threw themselves round their father's neck. The man had not known one happy hour since he had left the children in the forest; the woman, however, was dead.

Gretel emptied her pinafore until pearls and precious stones ran about the room, and Hansel threw one handful after another out of his pocket to add to them.

Then all anxiety was at an end, and they lived together in perfect happiness.

My tale is done, there runs a mouse; whosoever catches it, may make himself a big fur cap out of it.

Für Peter Handke

Einer, der aufsteht und Gedichte vorliest,ß
ist ein Vorlesender.
Einer, der aufsteht und Gedichte vorliest,
kann aber auch ein Dichter sein.

Einer, der aufsteht und Gedichte vorliest,
welche SEINE sind,
ist ein vorlesender Dichter.
So nennt man das.
Mit dem darf man nicht spaßen.

Weil, wenn einer,
der aufsteht und Gedichte vorliest,
Die SEINE EIGENEN sind, liest,
Dann sind die Besitzverhältnisse so,
Dass ein Verhalten zum Besitz abverlangt wird,
Worüber er nicht spaßen kann.

Weil ein Besitz etwas ist,
das sich überhaupt nicht zum Spaßen eignet.

Written by William Swann, published in *Die Zeit*, Nr. 22, 28 May 1971

Gliders

In the late 1940's Kirksey's grocery store got great stuff at the beginning of summer. Wax lips and teeth, big pink lips you could hold with your teeth. Big projecting teeth to slip over your incisors, smooth and soft once you warmed them up. Black wax mustaches you could hold in place by biting on a wax projection, the mustache so huge that it came down over your upper lip.

Yo-yos, sometimes even see-through yo-yos out of plastic, translucent yellow, with the string all curled up around the shaft. And tubes of colored sugar water that were whistles once you had drunk all the liquid out, well, sucked it out, there being a vacuum and you having to be careful not to collapse the wax walls by sucking too hard. All the neat stuff was out of wax, except the yo-yos of course.

And the gliders, the balsa wood gliders. They were there all year long, not seasonal. Sometimes one of the older boys would buy a folding-wing balsa glider, really expensive, the kind you launched with a rubber band sling, high high up, where at the top of the rise the wings would snap open and the plane would fly so far you might not find it sometimes, or it would land high up in a tree and you'd have to throw rocks at it to get it down. Of course, this at times would destroy the airplane.

When Kirksey got older, he realized some men did that with their love. He'd seen it far too often. Destroy love to get it back, to get the airplane down. "We had to bomb the hamlet to save it." The rock had been well intentioned, it just broke the wing off, or crushed the fuselage. And there it would be, spiraling down, gutshot, bumping into branches as it fell, ruined, angular. It wouldn't fly again, wouldn't trust again. Might get taken home to get taped up, might not. Wouldn't fly right ever again, anyway, being too heavy from the tape and out of line.

The nickel gliders were better in the long run, even though you couldn't fling them up so high. They lasted and lasted.

Jim Parrot's 1974 Chattanooga decision

IN 1974 AND 1975 I CLERKED FOR JUDGE JIM PARROTT ON THE TENNESSEE Court of Appeals. Judge Parrott's seven-page opinion was a painful decision. It made everyone in Chattanooga mad. My boss took a lot of heat. It was a necessary decision--as you will agree when you read it. I am proud of this decision, proud of my boss, and proud of me, because I wrote the opinion.

IN THE COURT OF APPEALS OF TENNESSEE
EASTERN SECTION

DECEMBER 12, 1974
JOHN A. PARKER, Clerk

STATE OF TENNESSEE, EX REL) FROM THE CIRCUIT COURT FOR
HAMILTON COUNTY

HON. DAVID TOM WALKER, JUDGE

-vs-

ROBERT STRICKLAND and

DEWAYNE STRICKLAND

EDWARD E. DAVIS and ROBERT BATSON OF CHATTANOOGA FOR
STATE OF TENNESSEE

JESSE O. FARR OF CHATTANOOGA FOR
ROBERT AND DEWAYNE STRICKLAND

<u>OPINION</u>

Parrott, J.

In this appeal we are concerned with whether two juveniles shall stand trial as adults.

Both the Juvenile and Circuit Courts of Hamilton County answered in the affirmative. We are unable to reach that result.

On February 12, 1973, Robert and DeWayne Strickland, fifteen and sixteen years of age, came under suspicion of an armed robbery and rape which had taken place the preceding evening. A number of detectives went to the Strickland home on the evening of February 12, picked up Robert and DeWayne, and took them to police headquarters for questioning. The youths denied any involvement in the incident. After inconclusive questioning, the boys were photographed, fingerprinted and released. This first session with the police lasted approximately from 11:00 p. m. to 3:00 a. m.

After further investigation, which included circulation of the youths' photographs, the police determined that more questioning was in order. On the afternoon of February 19, the police had DeWayne's high school coach bring him to headquarters; in response to a telephone call, Robert's parents brought him. This second session lasted--there is some disagreement in the record--around fourteen hours.

On both occasions, the Strickland boys were interrogated separately. At times the interrogation was intense, heated, loud and coercive in atmosphere. Although one or both of the Strickland parents were at the police headquarters the entire time, each boy underwent some questioning apart from a parent. The interrogations culminated the second night in each boy's indicating that he waived his constitutional rights.

"Their father," the brief for the State relates, "told them to tell the truth, and after their rights were read to them slowly, they never refused to speak and never asked for an attorney. At 10:45 p.m. on February 19, 1973, DeWayne waived his constitutional rights after they were repeatedly explained to him one at a time, and recounted his actions on the night of the crime.

... In a similar manner, at 12:55 a.m. on February 20, 1973, after four other juveniles including his brother had confessed, Robert Strickland waived his constitutional rights after going over them individually and also confessed his participation in the crime."

Only after these two sessions, held a week apart, had resulted successfully for the State, if we may use that phrase, were the two boys placed under the jurisdiction of the juvenile court.

A hearing was conducted in March in the Juvenile Court for Hamilton County which resulted in both boys being transferred to the Criminal Court of Hamilton County to stand trial as adults. (On May 11, 1973, a victim of the rape and armed robbery died; the charge of murder was added to the State's case.) An appeal of the transfer to criminal court was taken to the Circuit Court of Hamilton County, where a de novo review was held as to whether the statutory requirements for transfer from juvenile court had been met. The circuit court determined those requirements had been met, and the defendants have perfected this appeal.

The statutory requirements for transfer of a case from juvenile court are quite clear.

T. C. A. 37-234 requires that after a petition has been filed alleging delinquency, the court may, before hearing the petition on its merits, transfer a child to the sheriff of the county to be dealt with as an adult in the appropriate court. The child will be treated as an adult if four conditions are met. The statutory requirements are:

(1) the child was sixteen (16) or more years of age at the time of the alleged conduct; or the child was fifteen (15) or more years of age at the time of the alleged conduct if the offense charged included murder, rape, robbery with a deadly weapon or kidnapping;

(2) a hearing on whether the transfer should be made is held in conformity with §§37-224, 37-226 and 37-227;

(3) notice in writing of the time, place, and purpose of the hearing is given to the child and his parents, guardian, or other custodian at least three (3) days before the hearing;

(4) the court finds that there are reasonable grounds to believe that

(i) the child committed the delinquent act alleged;

(ii) the child is not amenable to treatment or rehabilitation as a juvenile through available facilities;

(iii) the child is not committable to an institution for the mentally retarded or mentally ill; and

(iv) the interests of the community require that the child be placed under legal restraint or discipline.

In this case it appears condition (1) was met in fact. Condition (3) was met in substance via actual notice. Condition (4) may or may not have been met. We would, however, like to register our dismay as to the State's cursory presentation of proof as to subhead (ii) of condition (4); i.e., amenability and existing facilities. The sufficiency of their case on both points is open to question. The record would seem to suggest that the State felt a trial as adults of these particular defendants could be obtained with only nominal attention to the statutory safeguards of condition (4).

The record, in its silence, discloses that condition (2) has not been met.

T.C.A. 37-234(a)(2) states that the juvenile hearing, on whether a transfer should be made to another court for the purpose of standing trial as an adult, must be held in conformity with T.C.A. 37-224, 37-226 and 37-227. Section 37-227 reads in pertinent part:

37-227. Basic Rights--Confessions--Sufficiency.--

(a) A party is entitled to the opportunity to introduce evidence and otherwise be heard in his own behalf and to cross-examine adverse witnesses.

(b) A child charged with a delinquent act need not be a witness against or otherwise incriminate himself. An extra judicial statement, if obtained in the course of violation of this chapter or which would be constitutionally inadmissible in a criminal proceeding, shall not be used against him . . . (emphasis supplied.)

It is apparent that the admissibility of the confession in this case raises serious constitutional questions. It is possible, for example, that the confessions were in no sense voluntary, but were exacted in an atmosphere of coercion from physically and emotionally spent suspects. There is the further question that these particular defendants may not have knowingly and intelligently waived their rights to counsel and silence, given their ages and decidedly subnormal mental development. Both are classed in the "borderline defective" range of mental capability.

Unfortunately, the State's inability to follow the prescriptions of the statutes does not require us to address ourselves to the questions of constitutional admissibility of the confessions obtained because those extra-judicial statements were "obtained in the course of violation of this [juvenile] chapter."

It will be seen that Sec. 37-227(b) is expansive in its protection of juveniles. Not only are they entitled to the constitutional rights of adults accorded juveniles of every state, In re Gault, 387 U.S. 1, 87 S.Ct. 1428, 18 L.Ed. 2d 527 (1967), they are also allowed to exclude any of their statements obtained in the course of violation of juvenile chapter of Tennessee. That means plainly and simply that the chapter must be tracked or the statements will be inadmissible.

It is clear from the record in this case that the requirements of the juvenile statute have not been adhered to. T.C.A. 37-215(a) states:

> 37-215. Custody--Release to proper party--Warrant for custody.
>
> (a) A person taking a child into custody, shall directly with all reasonable speed:
>
> (1) release the child to his parents, guardian or other custodian upon their promise to bring the child before the court when requested by the court, unless his detention or shelter care is warranted or required under §37-214; or
> (2) bring the child before the court or deliver him to a detention or shelter care facility designated by the court or to a medical facility if the child is believed to suffer from a serious physical condition or illness which requires prompt treatment. He shall promptly give notice thereof, together with a reason for taking the child into custody, to a parent, guardian, or other custodian and to the court. Any temporary detention or questioning of the child necessary to comply with this subsection shall conform to the procedures and conditions prescribed in this chapter and rules of court.

The Strickland boys were twice taken into custody for the purpose of questioning. Those custodies were lengthy. They were not brought before the juvenile court "directly with all reasonable speed." T.C.A. 37-215(a)(2). They were not in any sense "released" to their parents, T.C.A. 37-215(a)(2), by Mr. Strickland's following the boys to headquarters. And they were not the less in custody by virtue of their parents' presence at headquarters.

We believe the statute means what it says and the courts should not uphold efforts to circumvent its dictates. In clear language the statute requires that a child taken into custody shall be brought before the court in one of two ways: either by taking him there directly, or by having the parents bring him there when requested. Temporary detention or questioning is expressis verbis brought under the requirement.

It might be urged that T.C.A. 37-215(a)(1) provides for police interrogation by means of its reference to T.C.A. 37-214, which provides for detention or care required to protect the person or property of others, or because the child may abscond from the jurisdiction of the court. However, this argument fails due to T.C.A. 37-216, which designates approved places of detention and does not include detention in a police station:

37-216. Place of detention.--

(a) A child alleged to be delinquent or unruly may be detained only in:

(1) a licensed foster home or a home approved by the court;
(2) a facility operated by a licensed child welfare agency;
(3) a detention home or center for delinquent children which is under the direction or supervision of the court or other public authority or of a private agency approved by the court; or
(4) any other suitable place or facility designated or operated by the court. The child may be detained in a jail or other facility for the detention of adults only if other facilities in paragraph (3) above are not available, the detention is in a room separate and removed from those for adults, it appears to the satisfaction of the

court that public safety and protection reasonably require detention, and it so orders.

We hold that a hearing on the transfer of the Strickland boys to Hamilton County Criminal Court was not held in conformity with T.C.A. 37-227, as is required by T.C.A. 37-234.

Further, it must be noted that without the extra-judicial statements of the juveniles, which we have held to be inadmissible because they were obtained in violation of the juvenile chapter, there remains no evidence to support the circuit judge's findings that the defendants may be tried as adults. Thus, the circuit judge's findings and order cannot be permitted to stand.

It results the cause is remanded to the circuit court for proceedings not inconsistent with this opinion. For the reasons hereinabove given, the confessions shall not be used as evidence in any proceeding held under Title 37-101 et seq.

James W. Parrott, Judge

CONCUR:

Clifford E. Sanders, J.

Houston M. Goddard, J.

There was an earlier painful opinion in Chattanooga. It was in 1906.

Once again an opinion made everyone mad in Chattanooga. The opinion was written by Justice Holmes, but the critical grant of *habeas corpus* in the case was done by Justice Harlan. He was the one who took the heat, the one who was vilified by Chattanoogans.

United States v. Shipp, 203 U.S. 563, dealt with a lynching.

Ed Johnson, a black man, had been convicted in Hamilton County of the rape of a white woman, Nevada Taylor, at the trolley station at the base of Lookout Mountain. He was sentenced to death. 3 March 1906, Johnson's black lawyer, Noah Walter Parden, filed a writ of *habeas corpus*. He alleged that Johnson's constitutional rights had been violated.

Specifically, Parden argued that all blacks had been systematically excluded from both the grand jury considering the original indictment of Johnson and the trial jury considering Johnson's case.

Parden further argued that Ed Johnson had been substantively denied the right to counsel, because he, Parden, had been too intimidated by the threats of mob violence to file motions for a change of venue, a continuance, or a new trial. Parden argued Johnson had been deprived of due process and because of that was about to lose his life. And lose his life he did.

Parden was not the only hero in this sad story. Presbyterian minister T. Hooke McCallie, one of the first ministers of First Presbyterian Church on what is now McCallie Avenue, preached for peace from the pulpit and on the street. He later was one of the founders of the McCallie school on the McCallie family farm on Missionary Ridge. The McCallie family were all devout Presbyterians.

10 March 1906 Johnson's petition for *habeas corpus* was initially denied, and he was remanded to the custody of Hamilton County Sheriff Joseph F. Shipp, with the stipulation that Johnson have 10 days to file further appeals. His appeal to the Supreme Court was granted by Justice Harlan on March 17 and subsequently by the entire court on March 19.

However, even though advised of Harlan's *habeas corpus* ruling by telegram on 17 March--and the case and ruling being given full coverage by Chattanooga's evening newspapers that day--the case against Shipp and his chief jailer said that they had nonetheless allowed a mob to enter the Hamilton County Jail and lynch Johnson on the city's Walnut Street Bridge. The mob riddled him with bullets and pinned a note to his body: "To Justice Harlan. Come and get your nigger now."

The Supreme Court decided that the action constituted contempt of court because Sheriff Shipp, with full knowledge of the court's ruling, chose to ignore his duties to protect a prisoner.

Sheriff Shipp and several others were convicted of contempt of court. Shipp and two of his colleagues were sentenced to 90 days imprisonment, and three others were sentenced to 60 days imprisonment. In the court's words, "Shipp not only made the work of the mob easy, but in effect aided and abetted it."

However, when Shipp was released he continued to swear that he was innocent. He was welcomed back like a hero.

Threatened with violence, Noah Walter Parden had to leave the state, never to return.

February 2000, ninety-four years after the lynching, Hamilton County Criminal Judge Doug Meyer overturned Johnson's conviction, ruling that Johnson did not receive a fair trial because of the all-white jury and the judge's refusal to move the trial from Chattanooga.

June 17, 1953

THE EAST GERMAN UPRISING OF 1953 OCCURRED FROM 16 TO 17 JUNE. It began with a strike by construction workers in East Berlin against work quotas during the Sovietization process in East Germany.

Demonstrations in East Berlin turned into a widespread uprising against the government of East Germany and the Socialist Unity Party, involving an estimated one million people in about 700 localities. The protests against declining living standards and Sovietization policies led to a wave of strikes and protests that threatened to overthrow the East German government.

The uprising in East Berlin was violently suppressed by tanks of the Soviet forces in Germany, while demonstrations continued in more than 500 towns and villages for several more days before dying out.

In 1953, West Berlin renamed part of the Charlottenburger Chaussee *Straße des 17. Juni* to commemorate the uprising.

The uprising is commemorated in *"Die Lösung"*, a poem by Bertolt Brecht.

Die Lösung	The Solution
Nach dem Aufstand des 17. Juni	After the uprising of the 17th of June
Ließ der Sekretär des	The Secretary of the Writers' Union
Schriftstellerverbands	Had leaflets distributed on the
In der Stalinallee Flugblätter	Stalinallee
verteilen	Stating that the people
Auf denen zu lesen war, daß das Volk	Had forfeited the confidence of the
Das Vertrauen der Regierung	government
verscherzt habe	And could only win it back
Und es nur durch verdoppelte Arbeit	By increased work quotas. Would it
zurückerobern könne. Wäre es da	not in that case be simpler
Nicht doch einfacher, die Regierung	for the government
Löste das Volk auf und	To dissolve the people
Wählte ein anderes?	And elect another?

Katahdin and Grampa Young

KIRKSEY THOUGHT OFTEN GRAMPA YOUNG AND MOUNT KATAHDIN, of how they had driven in the summer of 1959 from Hancock, Maine, to Baxter State Park, there to sleep in sleeping bags on a wooden floor, three-sided campground shelter, and get up the next morning to take the Chimney Pond trail all the way to the top, the first place in the USA touched by the rising sun. How his grandfather had stopped to breathe several times during the climb. A moose had come down the trail just before the first glacial cirque. Kirksey and his grandfather had had to get off the trail, stand in the puckerbrush so the moose could go by slowly, massively. He had been so close Kirksey could have reached out and touched him.

He had never seen glaciation before, not so as to know what he was looking at. His grandfather told him the word "cirque," showed him with his hands how ice had made the bowl, had left a piled-up wall of boulders and gravel at the bottom edge of the outscooping, closing off the circle, and walling up deep clear snowmelt.

Kirksey and his grandfather climbed beside the cirque looking down into the water for what seemed hours, the beauty so intense. And then they were up and out of all the trees and brush, "above the timberline," he told himself, liking the sound of that, something from Jack London, though he knew it couldn't be elevation that caused the barren rock.

There had been stripes painted now and again on the rock to mark the trail. These gave way to cairns, piled one after another as they came out on the ridgeline leading to the summit. Another word his grandfather had known, a mastery word, an adventure word, an only-in-this-place word: cairn. That and "cirque" and "moraine" would be with Kirksey forever.

On top there had been clouds of fog, making the rock pyramids important, and then gray light, and then just as suddenly the weather changed. So quickly you knew you were close to heaven. Kirksey went back down the Knife Edge trail, his grandfather another, to meet in the campground, exhausted and wobbly in the fall of evening.

That had been the summer of 1959. In the winter that followed, Grandpa Young died, heart attack, the autopsy showing he had sustained an earlier event at some time. Had it been on the mountain? Or before then? Or after? Several years earlier, Grampa's Ellsworth doctor had prescribed "an ounce of whiskey every evening," which had delighted his grandfather, and had caused his grandmother to wonder about the doctor's good sense.

The lichens on Katahdin had been mustard yellow, gray, brown, crusty, blazes of color on bleak boulders. Kirksey had never seen lichens in such riot before: orange, arced, sprayed from nozzled cans, wiped on the rocks with painters' rags, speckled with brown here, there green mossy rashes on yellow smears.

On the very peak had been the biggest cairn of all, and a box for messages, and the pronouncement by sign that here was the end of the Appalachian Trail, so and so many thousands of miles to Springer Mountain, Georgia. Kirksey had thought, yes, that's true. It was stuff he knew, felt close to, believing that the AT was a part of who he was, a little seen, always sensed infinite meandering, a path of stitches sewing up America and stitching him to her, to her fogbound spruce, to wet granite, snowfalls, backpacks, gas stoves, small aluminum boxes ordered from REI, grommets, efforts at home-made pemmican. Kirksey was an American, stitched to the earth by this trail, by the thousands of miles he had hiked and was yet to hike, on this trail and others, knowing peace and wonder.

When his grandfather died, it had been a fact, no real grieving. Something to be dealt with. Still, he was gone, and they wouldn't do Katahdin again.

Kirksey and 1.36 tons of #89 stone

KIRSEY DROVE THROUGH THE MAZE AT VULCAN MATERIALS IN Sevierville. They dumped eleven inches of rock into his pickup bed. So far, so good. But on the spur back to Gatlinburg his truck was waddling, wobbling. It was clearly overloaded. Kirksey was surprised. He had thought his Ford King Ranch was invincible.

But that was only the beginning of his woes. In the driveway of the big house in Gatlinburg he began unloading. What he needed was a magic wand. What he had was a shovel. Three hours later, sunburned and whipped, he looked at the really quite modest pile of rock on the ground. Never again, he swore.

Kirksey and the dishwasher

KIRKSEY DIDN'T THINK HE WAS A FOOL, YET WHAT HAPPENED WITH HIM and the Gatlinburg dishwasher made him wonder.

He had run out of dishwasher pods. So he went halfway down the hill to a small market and picked some up. There was no choice, just one kind, made by Tide.

He put a pod in the dishwasher and turned it on. Pretty soon there was foam coming out under the door hinge on the front of the dishwasher. So much foam came out that it soaked the rug in front of the dishwasher. Kirksey figured he had improperly put a large mixing bowl in the dishwasher. So he rearranged the mixing bowl and started over.

It was no better. More foam came out. Kirksey kept sopping up the foam with paper towels until the wash cycle ended. The dishes were clean so he took them out and stored them away.

The next day Kirksey had another load of dishes to wash so he put in a pod and experienced the exact same thing again. At this point he decided he should call Diana.

She immediately told him that Tide pods were for washing clothes, not dishes. She said he should run the dishwasher many times with no dishes until he had rinsed all the Tide from the dishwasher system. Kirksey did this. Then he bought real dishwasher pods from Food City and all was well.

Kirksey found it interesting that he had come up with an intelligent, alternative, and completely incorrect explanation for the misbehavior of the dishwasher; it had had nothing to do with the placement of the mixing bowl.

Diana told him later that grocery stores made sure laundry products were in one aisle and dishwashing products in a completely different aisle. Kirksey thought this seemed to indicate that other men had made the same mistake. Perhaps even women.

Kirksey's father taught him to shoot

Not every sort of gun, but shotguns definitely. This was at the Knoxville Rod and Gun Club: 16-yard trap and handicap. Kirksey also took turns as a loader in the trap houses, placing clay targets on the powerful, dangerous arm which flung one (or in doubles, two) targets on the command of the scorer.

When Kirksey was in junior high school, 1954 to 1956, his father took him to the Athletic House. Kirksey's father thought it was time Kirksey had a rifle.

Kirksey had just come back from Boy Scout Camp Pellissippi in Anderson County. He had won the camp's marksmanship award. It turned out Kirksey was a natural with a rifle. More on that award in a moment.

The rifle he had used at camp was a single-shot .22. The camp had ten of them. Firing was from the prone position. After a few days Kirksey put a group of five through one hole. True, the hole was slightly larger than what just one .22 slug cuts out, but not by much. His instructor, who was Persian, was astounded. He said that the very slight enlargement of the hole was "probably due to the rotation of the Earth." That sounded pretty good to Kirksey at the time, good enough that he believed it.

The award from the instructor was a pin-on Iranian flag. Kirksey put it on his uniform right away, being careful not to stick himself. Kirksey still has it today, along with his merit badge sash. The Persian instructor could not make the English "th" sound, pronouncing it "t." All the campers loved hearing him say "my turd week at Camp Pellissippi."

The vagaries of history, of course, make Kirksey's teacher's award, his kindness, and his instruction particularly precious today.

Anyway, Kirksey's father was impressed enough that he put more guns into his hands. He bought Kirksey a thirty-two inch full choke single-shot Ithaca 12-gauge. That's the gun which had set the world's record for consecutive broken targets.

Kirksey has two shotguns now, five rifles, and four handguns, but his favorite gun of all is his Marlin lever-action .22, the one his father bought him at the Athletic House. Kirksey didn't know then that it was Annie Oakley's gun. Of all his guns, this is the one Kirksey will give to his child or grandchild who turns out to be the best shot.

Kirksey's dad did not introduce him to handguns, the third form of firearms. Kirksey took that up on his own and introduced his brother to it. That brother quickly surpassed Kirksey in handgunning but that brother never developed much skill in shotgunning. Kirksey also introduced his brother to spin fishing, and the brother before long surpassed him there as well.

Of course, Kirksey was competent with a BB gun, the fourth form of firearms, and his brother was an extraordinary shot with a pellet gun, the fifth form of firearms.

Kirksey and three colors of bear tags

IN THE GREAT SMOKY MOUNTAINS NATIONAL PARK, EUTHANASIA IS always the last option for bears. The first effort is to capture the bear and release it elsewhere within the park. That leads to a green tag. From then on it is green to yellow to red, a three-strike system.

The second time he is encountered, he gets a yellow tag. The third time he gets a red tag. When and if he is encountered wearing a red tag, his game is over. He can't be relocated. That just exports the problem. So it is time for him to go to heaven.

Regardless of whether he is on the tag system or not, every bear found scavenging on human remains is killed.

Kirksey and using things up

KIRKSEY WAS CHEAP. IT WAS BECAUSE HE WAS SCOTCH-IRISH. HE WOULD not waste. He would not discard a jar or a squeeze bottle with any contents he had paid for.

There was a tangible joy in finishing something. He knew this was essentially silly. But that was who he was.

It was the same thing with repairing an object. He would repair and repair rather than replace the thing. It was the satisfaction of getting more use from something. Scotch-Irish.

Kirksey's mother got a sun lamp for Christmas

KIRKSEY HAD THE JOB OF PUTTING UP THE CHRISTMAS TREE EACH year. His brothers were not old enough to help. The family did not have a tree stand, so Kirksey would make one out of a bucket of wet sand. But first he would cut a half inch off the stump of the tree so that it could drink water from the sand. And he would add water to the sand from time to time.

The lights went on first. Hot pointy ones, the kind where when one burns out, the whole string goes dark. Then the decorations went on, including the star on top. Some Christmases Kirksey would spray snow from an aerosol can on the branches. Last of all the tinsel, in individual strands laid on.

Kirksey was maybe fourteen or fifteen years old. It doesn't really matter when it was. The sun lamp happened. Kirksey's father gave his wife a sun lamp. It was all wrapped up, a big thing, four and a half feet tall. Kirksey's mother got the paper off. There was a black hood on top and a black heavy base on the floor. Kirksey's mother was delighted. "Oh, a hair dryer!" she said.

"No, damnit," said Kirksey's father. "It's a sun lamp."

"Well," said his mother, "You can use it for a hair dryer."

His father said, "Shit. Open something else."

Kirksey didn't know where his right foot was

MOST OF THE TIME. HE HAD TO LOOK DOWN TO KNOW. THE STRYKER corporation had done that to him. Oh, they hadn't meant to. It was just that they had produced a metal-on-metal femur and ball socket, and his doc, an excellent surgeon at the Knoxville Orthopedic Clinic, had used it. After two and a half years, Kirksey had cobaltism (metal poisoning), a failed right hip replacement, abductor avulsion, and a pseudotumor.

Kirksey talked to his doc about what to do. He was willing to do the "revision" of Kirksey's hip, but he did not want to. He said revisions were difficult, and should be done by someone who did a lot of them. So Kirksey went to the Mayo Clinic in Rochester, Minnesota, to a surgeon who did six or more revisions every week. That doctor found all of the above, grey rotted muscle, and a smelly mess. He put in a Johnson & Johnson hip.

Stryker then paid Kirksey a little money as part of a class action lawsuit. There were a lot of bad Stryker hips out there. But Kirksey wanted his leg back.

Kirksey gave money to panhandlers

On roadsides, most usually at the onramps to the interstate.

He hadn't always done it. For a while Kirksey had accepted the line that people deserved where they were in life. To give them charity was to subsidize laziness.

Kirksey remembered a panhandler in front of the Knoxville S&W Cafeteria. He was on the sidewalk, leaning against the wall. This was in the 1970's. The man had no legs. He had a skateboard affair, sort of a platform. His eyes were rheumy, glazed over white. He had a hat in front of him on the sidewalk. There was money in it. There was a sign around his neck. It read, "Also deaf."

Kirksey wished now he could go back in time and put money in the hat, a lot of money.

Honesty 1

In Hyde Park outside Boston, Kirksey had been stealing from the family grocery money. If he had been old enough, he might have called it creative diversion of the grocery money his mother gave him.

His mother would send him to a tiny grocery three blocks away. The purchases were always small: a loaf of bread, three onions, meat of some kind. Milk was delivered to the door by the milkman, so Kirksey never had to buy milk.

Kirksey would get home with the purchases, give his mother the change, and all would be well.

But one day his mother said, "That man is cheating you again. We'll just go see about this." He and his mother went to the store. She was carrying the bag with the purchases.

The grocer said, "Yes, three onions, liverwurst, Merita bread, and six pieces of candy." "Oh," said Kirksey's mother, looking at him. They went home.

When Kirksey's father got home, his mother told him what Kirksey had been doing. His father told him to get his piggy bank. The bank was of yellow glass, with a slot on top to get the pennies out. Kirksey's father made him get all the pennies out and give them to him.

Kirksey's mother was crying. Kirksey was crying. No more dishonesty for Kirksey. Ever.

Honesty 2

WHEN KIRKSEY WAS A JUDGE, HE HAD PERSONAL STAMPS FOR PERSONAL mail. He did not put his own correspondence into court mail.

But when he retired he took an old creaky wooden chair. He had put his briefcase onto it every day for thirty-two years. It was his friend.

Kirksey thought its previous life had been for alternate jurors. That didn't matter. What did matter was that Kirksey was taking a piece of public equipment. He could have written a check to someone pay for the chair, but he didn't. That seemed excessive, even talmudic.

Kirksey hated yellow jackets

TWO HAD GOTTEN HIM YESTERDAY. OR MAYBE IT WAS ONLY ONE THAT had stung him twice. He couldn't tell. Yellow jackets don't die when they sting. They inject venom and then withdraw, to fly away, to sting you again another day.

The honeybee can only sting once. Her stinger attaches to you and pulls out a good portion of her abdomen. So she dies. It is a suicide mission.

Kirksey couldn't see God's plan here. Honeybees were valuable. As far as Kirksey could see, yellow jackets were worthless.

The Buffalo nickel

The Buffalo nickel was struck by the United States Mint from 1913 to 1938. It was designed by sculptor James Earle Fraser.

In 1911 Taft administration officials decided to replace Charles E. Barber's Liberty Head design. They were impressed by Fraser's designs showing a native American and a bison.

The designs for the Buffalo nickel were approved in 1912, but were delayed several months because of objections from the Hobbs Manufacturing Company, a maker of mechanisms to detect slugs. The company was not satisfied by changes made in the coin by Fraser, but in February 1913, Treasury Secretary Franklin MacVeagh issued the coins.

Despite attempts by the Mint to adjust the design, the coins proved to strike indistinctly, and be subject to wear. Dates were easily worn away. In 1938, after the expiration of the minimum 25-year period during which the design could not be replaced without congressional authorization, the Jefferson nickel replaced the Buffalo nickel.

Fraser's design is admired today, and has been used on commemorative coins and the gold American Buffalo series.

Our nation's first major gold rush occurred not in California in 1849 (before California statehood), but in northeast Georgia, east Tennessee, and western North Carolina in 1828. At that time, especially in the underdeveloped southeast, commerce was achieved by subsistence farming and barter and few, if any, coins were available.

The year 1828 saw considerable expansion in southeastern gold mining, but the only US Mint was in Philadelphia and the transportation of gold dust and nuggets by stagecoach to the Philadelphia Mint was dangerous and slow.

Christopher Bechtler, a German born metallurgist and watchmaker, immigrated to the US in 1829 with his sons Augustus and Charles, and moved to Rutherfordton, NC, in 1830 where he started a jewelry and watch repair business.

Soon thereafter, miners began asking Bechtler to assay their gold dust and nuggets and convert it to coin. Bechtler was agreeable and began advertising his services for assaying and minting $2.50 and $5.00 gold coins at his own minting facility several miles north of Rutherfordton. Bechtler was known for his honesty and fairness. Each coin, though undated, was stamped on one side with the weight, purity (in carats), and dollar value. The other side of each coin was stamped with the Bechtler name and the geographical origin of the gold content.

Christopher Bechtler and his son, Augustus, minted territorial gold coins from 1831 until 1847 including the first gold dollar struck in the US. The US government never acknowledged the legitimacy of Bechtler gold even though the purity level in Bechtler gold often exceeded the purity of US minted gold coins.

Even after the demise of the Bechtler mint, Bechtler coins were accepted in commerce for many years, extending through the Civil War. Bechtler gold coins were hoarded in the South and traded at a premium. From 1831 to 1840, it is estimated that the Bechtler operation handled 40 percent of the total gold coin output nationwide. Though simple in design, Bechtler coins bore accurate descriptions of their weight and purity. Today, Bechtler gold is scarce and is sold and collected at premium prices.

Kirksey knew God made the clouds

THE QUESTION WAS, WHY DIDN'T HE PAY MORE ATTENTION TO THEM? Maybe because he had them all the time? So he took them for granted? He did not take roses for granted. Was that because he did not have roses all the time? Was that it?

Then he thought, we take some people for granted because they are always around. "Yes, they're wonderful people. Yes, we love them." But we treat them as part of the landscape.

Perhaps, he thought, clouds can be a lesson to behave better to the people around us.

Kirksey knew that he dressed for others

HE DID IT BECAUSE IT MET THEIR EXPECTATIONS. HE WANTED TO GIVE them what they were anticipating. He knew that if he did less than dress properly it would confuse the others. They could think, "*Well, here's Kirksey, and he looks like a slob. He doesn't care what impression he makes.*"

Kirksey felt it was not an exaggeration to say that it honored people to dress for them. If he did less than what was expected of him there would be an effect, and not a good one.

Then there was that whole thing about hats inside the house, inside a restaurant, even--horrors!--baseball caps. Of course, Kirksey knew there was no logical reason not to wear anything you wanted on your head whenever and wherever you went. But there it was. You just didn't do it.

Kirksey owned 50 acres in South Knox County

HE HAD OWNED IT FOR DECADES. IT WAS A SQUARE SOUTH-FACING RIDGE with eight acres of flat land at the bottom with grass. One of the neighbors asked whether he might grow hay there for himself and Kirksey had been delighted. The neighbor cut hay for several years and then moved away.

The eight acres grew up with bushes and small trees and then larger trees. The hilly forty-two acres extended all the way to the ridgetop and over the back. The highest point had a view of Mount LeConte. Kirksey at one time had considered building a house, but it was so remote Diana did not like the idea. So the land went unattended.

Kirksey learned his land had turned into a dump for household trash. That made no sense because there was a free, tax-supported Knox County dump center two miles away. But some people thought it was preferable to offload garbage onto Kirksey's land--old tires, broken plastic toys, plastic sheets, beer bottles, bags of household garbage, garden hoses.

Kirksey learned of this when a crew from Knox County went out and cleaned up one pile near the road, sent him a bill for it, and placed a lien on the fifty acres to assure payment of the cleanup cost. That got Kirksey's attention.

Kirksey went out with a friend and worked all day cleaning up more of the trash. Then he fenced the land and put up *no trespassing* signs.

A good thing which came out of the experience was that he met new neighbors, delightful people. They had a sign on their picket fence reading, *"Gardener wanted. Must look good bending over."*

He also met Ray Sexton as he was planting potatoes. Kirksey and Ray talked about gardening that day, and many days thereafter. As the summer went on, Ray shared his zucchini, his yellow squash, his cucumbers.

Kirksey's father and Camp Kilmer

LOCATED IN CENTRAL NEW JERSEY, CAMP KILMER WAS A FORMER United States Army camp that was activated in June 1942 as a staging area and part of an installation of the New York Port of Embarkation. The camp was organized as part of the Army Service Forces Transportation Corps. Troops were quartered at Camp Kilmer in preparation for transport to the European theater of operations in World War II. Eventually, it became the largest processing center for troops heading overseas and returning from World War II, processing over 2.5 million soldiers.

It officially closed in 2009. The camp was named for Joyce Kilmer, a poet killed in World War I while serving with 69th Infantry Regiment. He wrote "Trees":

> I think that I shall never see
> A poem lovely as a tree.
> A tree whose hungry mouth is prest
> Against the earth's sweet flowing breast;
> A tree that looks at God all day,
> And lifts her leafy arms to pray;
> A tree that may in Summer wear
> A nest of robins in her hair;
> Upon whose bosom snow has lain;
> Who intimately lives with rain.
> Poems are made by fools like me,
> But only God can make a tree.

When Kirksey's father was temporarily on the west coast, he wanted to let his wife know that he would soon be on the east coast at Camp Kilmer, where they might see each other. But he was forbidden by the Army to tell her that. So he sent her a telegram with one word, "Trees." It didn't work. Kirksey's mother didn't figure it out.

Kirksey's granddaughter and the octopus

WHEN MARREN LEARNED THAT THE OCTOPUS HAS THREE HEARTS, SHE said, "He must be able to love so much more than we can." Kirksey melted at her unsullied naivete.

The reason for the octopuses' impressive cardiac system is probably the unusual composition of their blood. Unlike vertebrates, which have iron-rich hemoglobin packed into red blood cells, octopuses have copper-rich hemocyanin dissolved directly in their blood. This means their blood is blue.

Hemocyanin is less efficient than hemoglobin as an oxygen transporter. The three hearts compensate for this by pumping blood at higher pressure around the body to supply the octopuses' active lifestyle.

Kirksey wondered about darkness

WAS IT SENTIENT? DID IT HAVE EMOTIONS? IF SO, PERHAPS IT GOT bored being shut up in the closet. It might want to get out. That would be reasonable.

How could it get out? Maybe it could become a liquid. If it could do that, it would not have to open the closet door. The darkness could simply flow out under the closet door. It could flow out under the door and across the floor.

If all the darkness flowed out of the closet, what would be left behind? A vacuum? No, not possible. Air would be sucked in under the closet door. There wouldn't be a vacuum.

But, if all the darkness flowed out, would it be light inside the closet? Maybe. Kirksey did not know. He was sure, however, that it was dark inside electric refrigerators when you shut the door. Reasonably sure.

The Greek Gods

IN THE WORLD OF THE GREEK GODS, THE WORLD OF HOMER, INDIVIDUAL
initiative is a crapshoot. You are the plaything of the gods.

You have been brought up to do offerings, rituals, and pour out fluids.
You believe these propitiations are necessary. But the gods are going to
do what the gods are going to do regardless.

In the world of Homer, "Man proposes, but it makes no difference." If
Zeus or Hera or Athena is calling the shots, you don't run the game.

Kirksey wondered about eating books

THE TOOTH FAIRY HAD GIVEN HIM THREE BOOKS TO EAT. NOT TO BITE, chew, and swallow, but just to place against his head so that all the content would go into his understanding. Everything that had been inside the books would then be inside him.

Kirksey wondered what he would choose. Kirksey thought probably one of them should be a foreign language textbook, a big one so that he would really master the language. But then he thought, okay, which language? And then he wondered if he really wanted to expand to new languages. He was already fluent in German, and his Spanish was pretty good. Wouldn't it be better to build out one of those two languages? He didn't know.

He also thought about the Oxford English Dictionary. He could hold it against his head and know everything that was in there. But did he really want to know that much about the history of the English language? He certainly didn't need the OED for vocabulary. Kirksey's vocabulary was already super.

What about the Bible? That might be an excellent choice, because Kirksey had a lot to learn there. How about the latest volume of *The Joy of Cooking*? Kirksey was a pretty good cook but he only did a few dishes. That sounded pretty good. What about an up-to-date atlas of the world? Countries were changing their names all the time now, and Kirksey was way behind. What about the complete works of Shakespeare?

So, he had two of the three at any rate: *The Joy of Cooking* and the Bible. But what about that language? Wouldn't it be cool to pick up Mandarin or Arabic? And what about that atlas of the world? What about the works of Shakespeare? He would have to think about it. Maybe he could go back to the Tooth Fairy and ask for six books.

Kirksey wondered about
the football itself

KIRKSEY HAD BEEN THINKING ABOUT THE GAME OF FOOTBALL. WHAT if the ball were different? What would happen?

Say, change it to a soccer ball.

The kicking game would improve. The passing game would not. Passing would still be possible, but catching a soccer ball on short quick passes would be harder than catching a normal football. Long passes would be easier to break up than passes done with a normal football. With runs, the ball could be held with one hand, but for security it would have to be held with two hands. That would slow the run game down. The game might simply become a kicking game, with field goals galore.

Or, change it to a tennis ball. What would happen? Unless the kicker's footwear were changed to something akin to a tennis racket, the kicking game would be strange: punts would be erratic, next to impossible, and kickoffs would be shorter, leading to fewer touchbacks. The passing game would improve because the ball would be easy to throw accurately. There would be virtually no fumbles, so the run game would improve.

But say the ball became a ping pong ball. What would happen? Assuming the kicker could equip his shoe with a ping-pong paddle, it would be possible to do kickoffs longer than ten yards, so all would be well there. Field goals would degrade hugely. The passing game would be difficult, next to impossible. There would be no fumbles, so the run game would be the go-to option.

Say the ball became a golf ball. What would happen? Assuming that the kickers could wear fancy footwear, choosing each shoe into the desired golf iron, the kicking game would blossom. Touchbacks on kickoffs, if that's what was wanted. Or high hang times, for tackles to be made close to the goal line. The passing game would probably degrade, due to drops and interceptions. The run game would be massive because there would be no fumbles.

Kirksey's grandmother had blue willow china

AND KIRKSEY HAD ALWAYS LOVED IT. BUT EFFIE HAD DIED YEARS AGO, and now when Kirksey thought back, he realized that Effie's blue willow had meant tea time, and that tea time had meant neighbors would drop in. Kirksey saw now that this was an extended community absent nowadays.

So what? His love for the Blue Willow was there just the same. Kirksey had bought some in honor of Effie. He had it in his big house in Gatlinburg. Some of his blue willow in Gatlinburg was old: Kirksey had inherited that from his mother, Effie's daughter Jeanette. But the best of Kirksey's blue willow was new, Johnson Brothers china, bought on the internet.

Kirksey had learned about blue willow's long manufacturing history. He had also learned that the pattern told an involved and not very happy story:

> Long ago, in the days when China was ruled by emperors, a Chinese mandarin, Tso Ling, lived in a magnificent pagoda under branches of an apple tree. There was a bridge down the hill from his pagoda. A wispy willow tree drooped over the bridge. Tso Ling was the father of a beautiful girl, Kwang-se. He had promised her as a bride to an old and wealthy merchant. She, however, fell in love with Chang, her father's clerk. She and Chang eloped across the sea to a cottage on an island. Tso Ling pursued and caught them. He was about to have them killed when the gods transformed them into a pair of turtle doves. The birds now fly high in the sky next to Tso Ling's apple tree.

Even though blue willow has a Chinese look and story, it was actually created in England in 1780 by engraver Thomas Minton. Minton then sold the design to potter Thomas Turner who mass-produced the pattern on earthenware. This became known as chinoiserie, European interpretations of Chinese decorative styles.

Blue willow began as transferware. Designs were transferred rather than hand-painted. Eventually blue willow became prime working-class dinnerware, made by 500 different makers.

The "Blue Plate Special" started at diners in the 1920's. It typically featured a big meal for a low price, served up on a blue plate. Many believe that the preferred dish was the blue willow "grill plate" which had separated areas for an entree and sides.

Johnson Brothers blue willow is now available in a twenty-piece set for $134.99 from Bed Bath & Beyond. It is simply gorgeous.

Kirksey's mother had a fantasy

KIRKSEY'S MOTHER JEANETTE WAS THE OLDEST OF FOUR CHILDREN. HER mother Effie called upon Jeanette to wash dishes after every meal. Jeanette did it, pretty much gladly, year after year. There was a window above the kitchen sink. Jeanette told Kirksey that she often thought about throwing the dishes out the window.

Love

In the sixth book of the Old Testament the Moabite Ruth says to her Israelite mother in law:

> Where you go I will go, and where you stay I will stay.
> Your people will be my people and your God my God.
> Where you die I will die, and there I will be buried.
> May the Lord deal with me, be it ever so severely, if even
> death separates you and me.

In 1958, Felice and Boudleaux Bryant described love this way for the Everly Brothers:

> Darling you can count on me
> 'Til the sun dries up the sea
> Until then I'll always be
> Devoted to you
>
> I'll be yours through endless time
> I'll adore your charms sublime
> Guess by now you'll know that I'm
> Devoted to you

Goethe treated love this way in 1774:

> Es war ein König in Thule,
> Gar treu bis an das Grab,
> Dem sterbend seine Buhle
> einen goldnen Becher gab.
> Es ging ihm nichts darüber,
> Er leert' ihn jeden Schmaus;
> Die Augen gingen ihm über,
> So oft er trank daraus.
> Und als er kam zu sterben,

Zählt' er seine Städt' im Reich,
Gönnt' alles seinen Erben,
Den Becher nicht zugleich.
Er saß beim Königsmahle,
Die Ritter um ihn her,
Auf hohem Vätersaale,
Dort auf dem Schloß am Meer.
Dort stand der alte Zecher,
Trank letzte Lebensglut,
Und warf den heiligen Becher
Hinunter in die Flut.
Er sah ihn stürzen, trinken
Und sinken tief ins Meer,
die Augen täten ihm sinken,
Trank nie einen Tropfen mehr

There was a king in Thule,
Was faithful till the grave,
To whom his mistress, dying,
A golden goblet gave.
Nought was to him more precious;
He drained it at every bout;
His eyes with tears ran over,
As oft as he drank thereout.
When came his time of dying,
The towns in his land he told,
Nought else to his heir denying
Except the goblet of gold.
He sat at the royal banquet
With his knights of high degree,
In the lofty hall of his fathers
In the castle by the sea.
There stood the old carouser,
And drank the last life-glow;
And hurled the hallowed goblet

Into the tide below.
He saw it plunging and filling,
And sinking deep in the sea:
Then fell his eyelids for ever,
And never more drank he!

Salmon

THERE ARE FISH IN THE LARGER FAMILY OF *SALMONIDAE* WHICH ARE not salmon. They are trout, char, grayling, and whitefish.

Salmon are native in two places: tributaries of the North Atlantic and of the Pacific Ocean.

Typically, salmon are anadromous: they hatch in freshwater, migrate to the ocean, and return to freshwater to reproduce. (However, populations of several species are restricted to freshwater throughout their lives.)

Folklore has it that anadromous fish return to the exact spot where they hatched to do their spawning. Tracking studies have shown this to be largely true. Homing behavior depends on olfactory memory.

The commercially important species of salmon are:

Salmo

Atlantic salmon

Migratory anadromous salmon

Landlocked salmon, found in a number of lakes in eastern North America and in Northern Europe.

These are not a different species from the Atlantic salmon but have independently evolved a non-migratory life cycle.

Oncorhynchus

Chinook or King salmon, the largest of all Pacific salmon, frequently exceeding 30 pounds.

Chum or dog salmon. This species has the widest geographic range of the Pacific species. It is second only to the Chinook in size. Chum can reach 30 to 35 pounds, but have an average weight of 8 to 15 pounds.

Coho salmon range from 8 to 12 pounds. A coho will not be as orange-red as sockeye or king salmon.

Pink salmon, the smallest of the Pacific species, with an average weight of 3.5 to 4 pounds.

Sockeye salmon rarely exceed 1.2 feet in length. They feed on plankton filtered through gill rakers. (Kokanee salmon are the land-locked form of sockeye salmon.)

Salmon eggs are laid in freshwater streams at high latitudes. The eggs hatch into "alevin" (also called "sac fry"). The fry quickly develop into "parr" with vertical stripes. The parr stay for six months to three years in the natal stream before becoming "smolts," distinguished by bright, silvery color. Only 10% of all salmon eggs survive to the smolt stage.

Smolt body chemistry changes, allowing them to live in saltwater. Smolts spend a portion of their out-migration time in brackish water, where their body chemistry becomes accustomed to osmoregulation in the ocean. The change is hormone-driven, causing physiological adjustments in the osmoregulatory organs such as the gills, leading to large increases in the ability to secrete salt.

Anadromous salmon spend one to five years (depending on the species) in the open ocean, gradually becoming sexually mature.

Atlantic salmon spend between one and four years at sea.

Chinook and sockeye salmon spawning in central Idaho travel over 900 miles and climb nearly 7,000 feet from the Pacific Ocean.

The female salmon uses her tail to create a shallow depression, called a "redd." The redd may contain 5,000 eggs covering 30 square feet. One or more males approach the redd, depositing sperm over the roe. The female then covers the eggs by disturbing the gravel at the upstream edge of the depression before moving on to make another redd. The female may make as many as seven redds before her supply of eggs is exhausted.

In the Pacific Northwest and Alaska, salmon are keystone species. They support birds, bears, and otters. The carcasses of the salmon transfer nutrients to the forest ecosystem.

Grizzly bears catch salmon and carry them into adjacent areas. There they leave partially eaten carcasses. Bears leave up to half their salmon on the forest floor. The foliage of spruce trees up to 1,600 feet from a stream contain nitrogen from salmon.

Salmon is healthy due to high protein, high omega-3 fatty acids, and high vitamin D content. PCB (polychlorinated biphenyl) levels may be up to eight times higher in farmed salmon than in wild salmon.

Still, according to the Journal of the American Medical Association, the benefits of eating even farmed salmon outweigh any risks imposed by contaminants.

In Norse mythology, after Loki tricked the blind god Höðr into killing his brother Baldr, Loki jumped into a river and transformed himself into a salmon to escape punishment from the other gods. When they held out a net to trap him, he was caught by Thor who grabbed him by the tail, and that is why the salmon's tail is tapered.

Don't let the old man in

THERE IS A CLINT EASTWOOD VIDEO WITH LYRICS. THE BACKSTORY IS that Toby Keith asked Clint what he was doing the next day. Eastwood's schedule was jam-packed.

A 2009 song resulted. You can hear it and see it on YouTube. I urge you to stop reading right now and go to YouTube.

Billy Joel: Movin' Out

THIS IS A SONG ABOUT CAPITALISM.

> *Anthony works in the grocery store*
> *Saving his pennies for some day.*
> *Mama Leone left a note on the door.*
> *She said, "Sonny, move out to the country."*
> *Oh, but working too hard can give you a heart attack.*
> *You ought to know by now.*
> *Who needs a house out in Hackensack?*
> *Is that all you get for your money?*

Billy Joel does not go on to say what our proper goals should be. If not a house in Hackensack, then what? His other big hit, *Piano Man,* is no help.

However, he is much in favor of intercourse. Speaking about *Only the Good Die Young,* he said, "When I wrote *Only the Good Die Young,* the point of the song wasn't so much anti-Catholic as pro-lust. The minute they banned it, the album started shooting up the charts."

Fried eggs

KIRKSEY'S GRANDFATHER HAD TAUGHT HIM TO COOK. NO ONE ELSE had bothered up to that point. It hadn't occurred to them. But here he was, seven or eight years old, and he didn't know how to cook.

The first thing you had to do, almost the best part, was slap the top of the cookstove, fast and carefully, to see if it was hot enough. If it wasn't, which Kirksey always hoped, then you balled up a half sheet of newspaper and poked it down through the stove eye, and put kindling on top of the ball of paper, and struck one of the big red-and-white-headed matches, the ones from the box behind the door.

You struck the match on the stove top. It made a soft rasping sound and flared and smelled like cap pistols. You could watch the kindling catch fire down through the stove eye for a while, and then you had to put the lid back in place so it would get hot.

The small black skillet was the one to use. It went right on top of the stove eye over the place where the kindling was burning. The bacon grease was in the coffee can on the counter. What you needed was a whole tablespoon, rounded on top, one of the big spoons from the drawer.

The white, semi-soft, brown-speckled grease would start to melt in the skillet, getting clear as water around the edges of the lump, and the water would expand and expand, the lump sinking down and disappearing, until the whole pan bottom was covered with melted fat.

Then you could push it around with the pancake turner, or shake the skillet, but you had to use a pot holder if you did that. It was time to get the pot holder anyway, because you might have to move the skillet while you cooked the egg.

Kirksey's grandfather showed him how to break the egg open, and years later Kirksey taught his own children the same movements. He had never known how much mystery there was in doing it right, how close disaster was, a spreading technicolor puddle on the floor, or an over-cracked shell and yellow and white running through your fingers. Or that if you didn't tap the shell hard enough on the stove edge, you couldn't slowly and carefully open the doors with your thumb and let the yolk out. You'd have to push your thumbs in, and that's when like as not they'd go all the way into the egg and break the yolk, and you couldn't do sunny-side-up then. You'd have to do hard-fried, like for a sandwich at lunch.

Kirksey learned to deposit the egg softly on the warming bacon fat, and it would just sit there, the yolk magnificent, self-assured, glowing, a glistening peach half, convex like a hat crown or an upside-down oatmeal bowl, and you couldn't even see the white. It looked just like the bacon grease. You could see right through it to the black skillet bottom.

And then a little film of white would start to appear, like an image coming up in a photographic tray, just a suggestion, outlines coming, a picture of egg landscape emerging, the edge reaching to here, curving around to here, coming close in to the yolk down here. It was time to jiggle the skillet a little, make the yolk get more in the middle. It would move some, slide back some, move again, sort of stay.

And then the best part would come, sliding the pancake turner around the edges of the white, lifting them up while they bubbled and whispered and flapped up and down, hissing about being a beautiful egg, while turning brown and crispy in places, and the yolk starting to film over and get a duller yellow.

At this point you could change your mind on sunny-side-up and poke a little cut in the yolk and a puddle would leak out and flow over toward the hot bubbling edge of the white, fall off the cliff into the hot black bottomless ocean, and fry up light yellow, right next to the white, an annex, a different colored stepping stone off the white iceberg, a porch into the ocean.

Corn pone

GRANDFATHER SWANN MADE THIS PONE IN COVINGTON, GEORGIA. MY father and I kept it up in Tennessee. It is thin and crunchy.

> white or yellow corn meal (not self-rising)
> ½ tsp. salt
> cold water
> olive oil
> preheated 375-degree oven
> real butter to serve with the pone when it is done

Rinse and dry the griddle or skillet if it hasn't been used in a while. Scour it with a wad of paper towel, damp with olive oil. Put a small dollop of oil into the skillet and spread it around covering the entire bottom and sides up about half an inch. The batter will be so thin it will not climb the sides. The skillet or griddle needs to be significantly damp with oil. If there is too much, daub it up with a paper towel.

Put the meal into a medium large bowl. Start with four heaping serving spoons. Add the salt. Turn a cold faucet on slightly, and put the bowl under it for a moment. Mix the batter with one hand. Add water in dribs until it is a thick soup. Dump it onto the center of the griddle or skillet. Pat it down, spreading it out gradually to the edges, rotating the griddle or skillet. The batter should be quite soupy. Jerk the griddle or skillet left and right to spread the batter. If it doesn't reach the edges, mix another batch and dump it in the middle of the first one and pat it out. Repeat the jerk motion.

Make sure the oven is at 375 degrees. Bake for 20 minutes; check. It probably won't be done. It may need five more; check again. It may need another five. Cook until there is ample brown at the edges, and maybe at some of the thin spots.

Serve with real butter.

If taken out of the oven when it is just browning, the pone will be soft and chewable. It is better to wait until it is thin and crunchy.

Grits the right way

Ingredients:

- *one teaspoon of salt*
- *one quart of water*
- *butter (never margarine)*
- *one cup old fashioned, stone ground, slow cooking grits (never "five minute," or "quick cooking" grits)*
- *grated cheese or sour cream (optional)*
- *black pepper*

Bring the water and salt to a boil. Grits stick, so put some butter into the boiling water before you whisk in the grits. Turn the heat to low, and put a lid on the pot.

Don't touch anything for twenty minutes, then check the consistency. If it's too wet, keep cooking. When it is done, you can whisk in cheese or sour cream. If not that, whisk in some butter.

Pour into a bowl, dot with butter, and serve. Make sure freshly ground black pepper is on the table.

Lobster with scrambled eggs

Equipment:

bowl for mixing eggs
large cast iron skillet with cast iron lid
409 spray cleaner
paper towels for clean up

Ingredients:

2-3 live Maine lobsters, one and a quarter pounds or larger
12 eggs
salt and pepper to taste

Directions:

Break eggs into a bowl but do not scramble.
Heat skillet on stove top until very hot.
Have the cast iron lid ready in one hand.
Throw lobsters into the skillet with your other hand, dump the eggs in fast, and get that lid on.
When the thrashing stops, the dish is ready.
Correct the seasonings.

Preparation time: 8 minutes

Cook time: 4 minutes

Clean up time: half an hour; use paper towels

Necks and Assholes

KIRKSEY'S MOTHER HAD FOR YEARS ASKED FOR TURKEY DARK MEAT, only to astonish him in her eighties by telling him that she didn't really like dark meat. It was just that she knew her children liked white meat, so she chose dark for herself. Not even her husband, Kirksey's father, had suspected this, he not being given to introspection on the possibility of kindness in others, although he had on the topic of fried chicken accused his wife of preferring "necks and assholes."

This phrase, the exact words, had often surfaced to the delight of Kirksey and his siblings, the father at this point not being wholly intoxicated, though a sure portent of things to come, because it was so off-color. Yet Kirksey and his brothers knew their father was right. Their mother would always choose the scrawniest, least attractive chicken pieces for herself, those flawed either by anatomy or preparation, saying they were what she really wanted.

Kirksey had had a cousin who had brought her mother, then widowed, a pound of gizzards for her birthday, intending to fix them for her, only to learn that her mother disliked gizzards, had disliked them all her married years, and had only chosen the brown contortion from the platter so that her children and mate might have a wider choice.

Kirksey guessed it was a motherhood thing, not specifically Southern, although it was true the cousin's mother had been an Agnes Scott graduate, and that Kirksey's own mother had lived long enough in Georgia that she could well have learned it there.

Newt Gingrich, Dec. 21, 2020, on Biden's election

A SMART FRIEND OF MINE WHO IS A MODERATE LIBERAL ASKED WHY I was not recognizing Joe Biden's victory. The friend made the case that Mr. Biden had gotten more votes, and historically we recognize the person with the most votes. Normally, we accept the outcome of elections just as we accept the outcomes of sporting events. So, my friend asked why was 2020 different?

Having spent more than four years watching the left "resist" President Donald Trump and focus entirely on undoing and undermining the 2016 election, it took me several days to understand the depth of my own feelings.

As I thought about it, I realized my anger and fear were not narrowly focused on votes. My unwillingness to relax and accept that the election grew out of a level of outrage and alienation unlike anything I had experienced in more than 60 years of involvement in public affairs.

The challenge is that I, and other conservatives, are not disagreeing with the left within a commonly understood world. We live in alternative worlds. The left's world is mostly the established world of the forces who have been dominant for most of my life.

My world is the populist rebellion which believes we are being destroyed, our liberties are being cancelled, and our religions are under assault. Note the new Human Rights Campaign to decertify any religious school which does not accept secular sexual values, and that many Democrat governors have kept casinos open while closing churches though the COVID-19 pandemic.

In 2016, I supported an outsider candidate, who was rough around the edges and in the Andrew Jackson school of controversial assaults on the old order. When my candidate won, it was blamed on the Russians. We now know, four years later, that Hillary Clinton's own team financed the total lie that fueled this attack.

Members of the FBI twice engaged in criminal acts to help it along — once in avoiding prosecution of someone who had deleted 33,000 emails and had a subordinate use a hammer to physically destroy hard drives, and a second time by lying to FISA judges to destroy Gen. Michael Flynn and spy on then-candidate Donald Trump and his team.

The national liberal media aided and abetted every step of the way. All this was purely an attempt to cripple the new president and lead to the appointment of a special counsel, who ultimately produced nothing.

Now, people in my world are told it is time to stop resisting and cooperate with the new president. But we remember that the Democrats wanted to cooperate with Mr. Trump so much that they began talking about his impeachment before he even took office. The *Washington Post* ran a story on Democrat impeachment plots the day of the inauguration.

In fact, nearly 70 Democratic lawmakers boycotted his inauguration. A massive left-wing demonstration was staged in Washington the day after, where Madonna announced she dreamed of blowing up the White House, to widespread applause.

These same forces want me to cooperate with their new president. I find myself adopting the Nancy Pelosi model of constant resistance. Nothing I have seen from Mr. Biden since the election offers me any hope that he will reach out to the more than 74 million Americans who voted for President Trump.

So, I am not reacting to the votes so much as to the whole election environment. When Twitter and Facebook censored the oldest and fourth largest newspaper (founded by Alexander Hamilton) because it accurately reported news that could hurt Mr. Biden's chances, where were the *New York Times* and *Washington Post*? The truth of the Hunter Biden story is now becoming impossible to avoid or conceal.

The family of the Democrat nominee for president received at least $5 million from an entity controlled by our greatest adversary. It was a blatant payoff, and most Americans who voted for Mr. Biden never heard of it, or were told before the election it was Russian disinformation. Once they did hear of it, 17% said they would have switched their votes, according to a poll by the Media Research Center. That's the entire election. The censorship worked exactly as intended.

Typically, newspapers and media outlets band together when press freedom is threatened by censorship. Where was the sanctimonious "democracy dies in darkness?" Tragically, the *Washington Post* is now part of the darkness.

But this is just a start. When Twitter censors four of five Rush Limbaugh tweets in one day, I fear for the country. When these monolithic Internet giants censor the president of the United States, I fear for the country. When I see elite billionaires like Mark Zuckerburg spend $400 million to hire city governments to maximize turnout in specifically Democratic districts without any regard to election spending laws or good governance standards, I fear for the country. When I read that Apple has a firm rule of never irritating China, and I watch the NBA kowtow to Beijing, I fear for our country.

When I watch story after story about election fraud being spiked, without even the appearance of journalistic due diligence or curiosity, I know something is sick.

The election process itself was the final straw in creating the crisis of confidence which is accelerating and deepening for many millions of Americans. Aside from a constant stream of allegations of outright fraud, there are some specific outrages, any one of which was likely enough to swing the entire election.

Officials in virtually every swing state broke their states' own laws to send out millions of ballots or ballot applications to every registered voter. It was all clearly documented in the Texas lawsuit, which was declined by the U.S. Supreme Court based on Texas' procedural standing, not the merits of the case. That's the election.

In addition, it's clear that virtually every swing state essentially suspended normal requirements for verifying absentee ballots. Rejection rates were an order of magnitude lower than in a normal year. In Georgia, rejection rates dropped from 6.5% in 2016 to 0.2% in 2020. In Pennsylvania, it went from 1% in 2016 to .003% in 2020. Nevada fell from 1.6% to .75%. There is no plausible explanation other than that they were counting a huge number of ballots, disproportionately for Mr. Biden, that normally would not have passed muster. That's the election.

The entire elite liberal media lied about the timeline of the COVID-19 vaccine. They blamed President Trump for the global pandemic even as he did literally everything top scientists instructed. In multiple debates, the moderators outright stated that he was lying about the U.S. having a vaccine before the end of the year.

The unanimously never-Trump debate commission spiked the second debate at a critical time in order to hurt President Trump. If there had been one more debate like the final one, it likely would have been pivotal.

But any one of those things alone is enough for Trump supporters to think we have been robbed by a ruthless establishment, which is likely to only get more corrupt and aggressive if it gets away with these blatant acts. For more than four years, the entire establishment mobilized against the elected president of the United States as though they were an immune system trying to kill a virus. Now, they are telling us we are undermining democracy.

You have more than 74 million voters who supported President Trump despite everything, and given the election mess the number could easily be significantly higher. The truth is tens of millions of Americans are deeply alienated and angry. If Mr. Biden governs from the left, and he will almost certainly be forced to, that number will grow rapidly.

Given this environment, I have no interest in legitimizing the father of a son who Chinese Communist Party members boast about buying. Nor do I have any interest in pretending that the current result is legitimate or honorable. It is simply the final stroke of a four-year establishment-media power grab. It has been perpetrated by people who have broken the law, cheated the country of information, and smeared those of us who believe in America over China, history over revisionism, and the liberal ideal of free expression over cancel culture.

I write this in genuine sorrow, because I think we are headed toward a serious, bitter struggle in America. This extraordinary, coordinated four-year power grab threatens the fabric of our country and the freedom of every American.

Benjamin Cardozo is an embarrassment

BENJAMIN CARDOZO (1870-1938) SERVED ON THE NEW YORK COURT OF Appeals from 1914 to 1932 and on the U.S. Supreme Court from 1932 until his death. He is an embarrassment for any person who loves America as founded.

My own college (Harvard) and graduate school (Yale) being held hostage by leftism really wounds.

It is the decline of American values. My response is not to bemoan the loss of Harvard and Yale, but to persuade them to do better. I do not stay silent, even though I know I cannot perceptibly change the benighted places.

Harvard was founded in 1636. It was gloriously present at the founding of America. It now urges the foundering of America.

Cardozo is someone who doesn't care about the original intent of our founders. For him a judge is a philosopher king. Cardozo wants what he calls a "living law":

> Above all in the field of constitutional law, the method free decision sees through the transitory particulars and reaches what is permanent behind them. Interpretation, thus enlarged, becomes more than the ascertainment of the meaning and intent of lawmakers whose collective will has been declared.

> Courts are to search for light among the social elements of every kind that are a living force behind the facts they deal with. The power thus put in their hands is great and subject, like all power, to abuse; but we are not to flinch

from granting it. In the long run there is no guarantee of justice except the personality of the judge.

. . . no judge of a high court, worthy of his office, views . . . his place so narrowly. If that were all there was to our calling, there would be little of intellectual interest about it.

The Giving Tree, by Shel Silverstein

THIS IS A DISGUSTING STORY. IT URGES THAT THE "GENEROUS" TREE should be praised for giving away its body parts until nothing is left of it.

But in fact, the tree is not generous. It is stupid and abusive. It creates a dependency relationship with the man. The man loses his freedom in the same steps as the tree loses its body parts. The two become codependent and sick.

The boy is selfish. He never grows or learns in the story. He keeps taking from the tree until only a stump remains. The boy never matures. Even as an old man he remains a child, always taking, never giving. By the end of the story this man-child is alone. He takes care of no one, not even the tree. Instead, he sits on the stump, absorbed in misery and self pity, as the tree continues enabling this bad behavior.

This book should not be read by children or to children.

When I found this book with my own children, I immediately hated it. The book destroys personal worth and self-respect. It has no place in any library, except as an exhibit of dangerous writing.

Should it be burned? Of course not. It should be kept around as a warning.

Cat's In The Cradle, By Harry Chapin

CHAPIN SAID, "FRANKLY, THIS SONG SCARES ME TO DEATH." CHAPIN was right to be terrified. It is about the seduction of skipped opportunities. If you can listen to it and not cry, you are stronger than I am.

At the very start of the song, the father neglects his son. He is not interested in his birth. The boy comes into the world "in the usual way."

The seduction of skipped opportunities. *"I'll get around to it in due course. Not now. I have more important things to do right at this moment."* The father could read stories to his son about little boy blue and the man in the moon. But he doesn't. He moves on to the next task, the more important things. The boy grows up, the child of a succession of missed opportunities.

Think back to the horrible story by Shel Silverstein, *The Giving Tree*. I call it Exhibit One in the active destruction of children. But *Cat's in the Cradle* is about passive harm. The harm of not doing. In his not doing, the father replicates himself.

I say again, if you can listen to this song and not cry, you are stronger than I.

There is one hopeful thing here: The son speaks of his kids having the flu. So, here at least he is involved with his own children. Is it enough? By itself, of course not. But maybe, just maybe, he reads to them. I doubt it.

Guns in the USA

THE ANTI-GUN LOBBY USES STATISTICS TO MAKE A CASE AGAINST GUNS: *"Guns in America kill X number of people per year."* Guns are bad; something should be done: *"We must get rid of guns."*

According to the Centers for Disease Control, in 2019 there were 47,511 suicides. Of these, 23,941 were done by firearm. Which is half of all the suicides in the United States.

Ignoring the Second Amendment (which guarantees the right to keep and bear arms), you might believe the anti-gun position is appropriate. You would do this if you believe people should be stopped from killing themselves with guns. If that is your position, well and good. A modern libertarian (but not John Locke) would say the decision for or against suicide is personal. It is not something someone else should decide.

Additionally, there is another question: If guns should somehow be unavailable in the USA, how many of the 23,941 firearm suicides will seek alternate routes?

It is important to bear in mind that the anti-gun lobby's desire to remove guns is **premised on the idea that it can be done**. If the Democrat party somehow achieved a massive penal code for gun possession, then the only persons surrendering guns would be lawful people, most of whom pose no threats to anyone, except perhaps themselves (suicides). All the bad people--and most of the good ones--will keep their guns.

The desire to rid America of guns is also premised on trusting the government:

- to do the removal effectively,
- to protect us from bad guys once we are defenseless,
- and not to oppress us (Venezuela, Cuba, USSR, the Third Reich, Big Brother)

I would love to trust the government. The founding fathers did not. They believed an armed populace was the last protection against an oppressive government.

Let us remember that in 1935 Hitler spoke for his own government about guns: *"This year will go down in history. For the first time, a civilized nation has full gun registration. Our streets will be safer, our police more efficient, and the world will follow our lead into the future!"*

Printed in the United States
by Baker & Taylor Publisher Services